MUSTANG

A SOURCE BOOK

EDITED AND ANNOTATED BY

Robert C. Ackerson

Osceola, Wisconsin 54020, USA

Bookman Publishing/Baltimore, Maryland

Printed in the U.S.A.
Copyright 1984 in U.S.A. by Bookman Dan!, Inc.

ISBN 0-934780-41-2

First Edition
First Printing

Inquiries may be directed to:
Bookman Dan!, Inc.
P.O. Box 13492
Baltimore, Maryland 21203

Book trade distribution by:
Motorbooks International
P. O. Box 2
Osceola, Wisconsin 54020

Contents

A legend turns 20.

Get it together — Buckle up.

The 20th Anniversary Mustang

Twenty years ago the first Mustang rolled off the assembly line and made automotive history. The fun and excitement of that first year made Mustang a legend.

Now you can capture the spirit of the original in a limited edition Mustang GT. Available in convertible and 3-door models.

She's quick.

With a high output 5.0 liter V-8 engine. Five-speed gearbox. And six-way articulated driving seats.

She's fun.

Push a button, take a ride with the wind. The convertible has a real glass rear window, room for four and a power top.

She's rare.

Only 5,000 Limited Edition Mustangs will be built, so see your dealer soon. And ask about special Anniversary savings on selected Ford cars and trucks.

A sporty car makes it fun. But only Ford makes it Mustang.

The 20th Anniversary Mustang.

Have you driven a Ford... lately? *Ford*

4

It would be trite to describe the Mustang as the right car for the right time. Few cars were so perfectly groomed and matched for their prospective customers as was the original version. It was the Mustang that really zeroed in on the first crop of wartime babies who were looking for a sports car with four seats, reliability, performance and individuality. Other manufacturers had flirted with products that came tantalizingly close but none hit the bull's eye as did the Mustang.

To put the Mustang into a broader historical perspective is to regard it as the mid-sixties successor to three great cars from Ford Motor Company: the Model A Ford, the Continental Mark II and the original two-seater Ford Thunderbird. Adopting the Model A's "everyman's" personality, the Mustang's appeal was universal. People from all walks of life could relate to the Mustang. Moreover, like the Model A, the Mustang was a car that performed in a fashion belying both its low base price and humble origins. Both the Mark II and Thunderbird provided a solid styling heritage for the Mustang. These automobiles were near-flawless examples of the long hood, short deck format and if minor lapses on the part of their designers could be detected in some details, they paled in comparison to the cohesive and timeless forms that have enabled them to weather the years' passing with considerable grace.

Thus it is with the Mustang. Looking at that first Mustang flyer that appeared in my mailbox back on May 2, 1964, it's hard to believe that it's been fully two decades since the Mustang debuted. It, too, has been touched gently by time.

If the Mustang grew in size and power during its midyears to unnecessary proportions, so also did its peers. And if the Mustang II perhaps was a bit too down-sized for devotees of the original version, its successor was right on the money, a near perfect platform for a modern high performance automobile in the American idiom.

Twenty years later we're still in love with the Mustang. It remains an automobile that looks good, sounds good and whether it's fresh from the showroom or pushing 20, a Mustang seldom passes by unnoticed by this enthusiast.

Thus, writing about the Mustang really becomes a "going back home" type of adventure. But memories fade and facts and figures become fuzzy. Therefore, many sources were consulted in the preparation of this Source Book. Among those proving particularly useful were NADA guides, the very comprehensive Ford Buyer Guides, "Mustang, The Complete History of America's Ponycar," by Gary Witzenburg and "Fearsome Fords 1959-73," by Phil Hill. In addition, numerous issues of "Motor Trend," "Car and Driver," and "Road & Track" were consulted, along with press material from Ford Motor Company.

All of the individuals who contributed to this reservoir of information are extended a sincere "Thank You."

Schevenus, New York
June, 1984

1964-1966

The Mustang's appearance was distinctive without any recourse to sensationalism on the part of its designers. It was a hard car to dislike. A 108 inch wheelbase, overall length of 181.6 inches and 68 inch width promised a tailored, trim look that enjoyed instant recognition and provided the Mustang with its basic character for a full decade and beyond.

The short rear deck was further accentuated by the upsweep of its lower edge while a side body character line ending in a simulated air scoop underscored the placement of the Mustang's passenger compartment well back on its chassis. These proportions worked visual miracles. Few observers, for example, realized the Mustang and Falcon had identical overall lengths.

Close attention to details and restraint on the part of Ford stylists paid off in a unique front and rear view appearance. The back bumper was a simple affair with upswept ends whose form linked up with the rear fender line. Although they were actually fitted with a single lense, the use of a three-section bezel gave the Mustang's taillights the appearance of a more costly triple light set up. The fuel filler of the Mustang's sixteen gallon fuel tank was located midway between the taillights and the filler cap carried the Mustang logo surrounded by Ford Mustang lettering. The optional ($10.70) circular backup lights were mounted beneath the bumpers.

At the front, a high mounted grille opening had its full share of character elements. Against a honey-combed mesh background was a single horizontal bar whose intersection with a vertical spear was marked by the galloping pony that within just a few months was instantly identified as the symbol for one of the most likeable American cars of the postwar era. The finishing touch to what was almost unanimously regarded as an attractive automobile was a squared-off roof line for the Hardtop with just the proper amount of creases to avoid a sense of heaviness. The profile of the Convertible's top was virtually identical to the Hardtop's, in other words, the softtop Mustang looked good whether its top was up or down. Both models were offered in fifteen different exterior colors, ranging from Raven Black to Poppy Red.

One of the Mustang's keys to success was Ford's awareness that no American manufacturer ever launched a successful new car by having the word "cheap" sprawled (figuratively, of course) all across its interior and exterior. There never really was such a thing as a stripped Mustang. Included in the $2,368 base price of the Mustang Hardtop (the Convertible listed for $2,614) were such highly visible features as thin shell, deep foam bucket seats, padded instrument panel, full wheel covers, a color-keyed vinyl interior and wall-to-wall carpeting, a sports steering wheel, twin automatic courtesy lights, a glove box light and front seat belts.

The Mustang's deeply hooded instrument panel contained a horizontal speedometer reading to 120 mph, surrounded by circular gauges for fuel level and engine temperature. Directly beneath the speedometer, separated by the odometer, were warning lights for oil pressure and the generator. The windshield wipers and light switches were mounted on the lower surface of the dash to the left of the steering column, while the ignition and cigarette lighter were symmetrically located on the opposite side of the steering column. Controls for the optional radio were center positioned on the dash, while the heater/

defroster levers were placed between the cigarette lighter and ash tray. All Mustangs regardless of their transmission had a floor-mounted shifting lever.

Options for the Mustang abounded. The appeal of its interior could be enhanced by the purchase of the push button AM radio ($58.50 including antenna), a rear speaker ($11.95), the sports console ($51.50), padded sun visors ($5.70) and air conditioning ($283.20). For another $75.95 Ford offered a Rally Pac consisting of an electric tachometer reading to 6000 rpms and a 24 hour clock. These 2.5-inch diameter gauges were mounted on the steering column. Exterior dress-up options included either simulated wire wheels ($45.80) or knock-off wheel covers ($18.20) and, in place of the standard side indentation chrome embossing, an Accent Group option consisting of side striping and rocker panel molding was offered for $16.10. A vinyl roof for the Hardtop listed at $75.80, whitewalls retailed for $33.90 and backup lights were offered for $10.70.

The basic Mustang engine-transmission combination consisted of the familiar 101 hp, 170 cid, ohv six and a three-speed manual gearbox. For the first time, Ford offered its three-speed Cruise-O-Matic as an option with this engine for $189.60. Initially only two other engines were available for the Mustang. The frisky 164 hp, 260 cid V-8 was offered at $116 with either the three-speed manual or Cruise-O-Matic transmissions. The more costly ($181.70) 289 cid V-8 option was fitted with a Ford-built four-barrel carburetor and rated at 210 hp. Either Cruise-O-Matic or Ford's all-syncromesh four-speed priced at $188 could be linked to this V-8. In June Ford began offering Mustangs with the 271 hp, HP engine which was identical to that installed by Carroll Shelby in his Cobras. An outlay of $435.80 bought this engine with a stronger crankshaft, bearings, connecting rods and pistons. In addition, a considerably wilder 306 degree duration cam, a 10.5:1 compression ratio and a single Holley four-barrel were specified.

Although both the Mustang's platform type frame and suspension were closely related to those found on the Falcon, they performed their role well. For added strength, the convertible Mustang had front torque tubes and an additional steel panel welded to the rocker rail. In several areas heavier gauge steel was also specified. On both models box-section side rails were used, five crossmembers were installed and a heavy-gauge front stamping, welded to the side rails, enclosed the engine compartment to which the front fenders were bolted.

The simple and sturdy character of the Mustang frame was shared by its suspension. At the front were coil springs with concentric shock absorbers mounted to the upper control arm. An anti-roll bar was a standard equipment unit. At the rear three-leaf springs with a length of 53 inches were installed along with angled tubular shock absorbers. The primary differences between this arrangement and the Falcon's consisted of altered front spring mountings plus stiffer springs and rubber bump stops.

The Special Handling Suspension option substantially upgraded the Mustang's roadability. Heavy-duty shocks and stiffer front/rear springs were included, as was a larger (0.84 inch to 0.69 inch diameter) front anti-roll bar. In addition, faster 22:1 instead of 27:1 steering with 3.5 turns lock to lock was installed. Replacing the standard 6.50 tires and 13 inch wheels were 14x5 inch rims with 6.15x 14 tires or 15x5.5 inch wheels with 5.50/5.90

Firestone Super Sport tires.

Ford promoted the Mustang as the "first of the 65s" but those marketed from April to September 1964 are generally regarded today as 1964½ models. Total production of these first generation Mustangs was 121,538, of which 92,705 were Model 65A Hardtops and 28,833 were Convertibles with a 76A Model designation.

The Mustang galloped into 1965 at a full gait with its sales setting record after record. After 9 months of production over 250,000 had been assembled and by mid-July the Mustang was outselling the Falcon. The next month the only cars above the Mustang's sales level were the Chevrolet Impala and Ford Galaxie. In April the Mustang celebrated its first birthday with a first year production mark for a new American automobile of 418,812. No less spectacular was the 1965 model year production of 559,451 Mustangs. No wonder the 289 V-8 Mustang was voted the best Sports Sedan in the 2.5-5.0 liter class by the readers of "Car and Driver" magazine!

Ford undoubtedly could have stood pat with the Mustang for 1965 and sales would have continued to be sensational. But instead a substantial number of changes, virtually all for the better were incorporated into its design.

On September 25, 1965 a new fastback 2+2 model (body code 65A) joined the Mustang lineup. Taking full advantage of this body style on a short wheelbase automobile, its creators retained the basic Mustang look while extending the appeal of the nation's first pony car to even more buyers. Louvered air outlets on the rear quarter panels provided both an attractive element to the 2+2 exterior appearance as well as the advantage of flow-through ventilation for its occupants. A rocker panel trim strip was standard on the 2+2 and the side body identification read "Mustang 2+2." On all 1965 models the side Mustang lettering was slightly larger than in 1964.

Included in the 2+2's base price of $2,589 was a fold-down rear seat with an access door to the trunk area. This feature made the most of the Mustang's non-passenger carrying capacity, since the 2+2 trunk opening was quite narrow. Other standard interior features of the 2+2 were padded sun visors and small, circular courtesy lamps placed on each side of the rear side walls.

In April, 1965, the Mustang's attractiveness as a sports car took another step forward with the arrival of the $165.03 GT option. Available for all three body forms, the GT package had as its base engine-transmission package the 225 hp/289 cid V-8 and a three-speed, all-synchromesh gearbox. Straight-through dual exhausts with chrome "trumpet" extensions exited through the rear valance panel. Front disc brakes were also supplied.

Exterior identification of the GT equipped Mustang was well-coordinated and effective. Fog lights were inserted in the outer grille regions and a chrome grille lip molding was added. Lower body stripes with Mustang lettering plus a GT insignia behind the front fender wheel cutout replaced the standard Mustang body lettering and logo. Replacing the standard instrument panel with its pseudo-Falcon economy car look was an impressive arrangement consisting of a 140 mph speedometer bracketed on the left by gauges for fuel level and oil pressure. To its right were additional gauges for amps and engine coolant temperature. The popularity of this option was evident by its installation in over 15,000 Mustangs during the remaining portion of the model year. Common to all 1965 Mustangs was an adjustable

passenger seat. The seats for Convertible models were all-vinyl while those installed in the Hardtop and 2+2 were finished in cloth and vinyl.

With a total of sixteen exterior colors available for 1965, five of which (Tropical Turquoise, Twilight Turquoise, Ivy Green, Champagne Beige and Honey Gold) were new, most observers barely noticed that the only change of consequence to the Mustang body design consisted of the elimination of the stiffening flap on the outer corners of the hood. Although the base price of the Hardtop (body code 65A) and Convertible (body code 76A) rose slightly to $2,372 and $2,614 respectively, Ford could hardly be accused of price gouging. In fact the use of a larger 200 cid, 120 hp, 7-main bearing six as the Mustang's standard engine more than justified this small price increase. Three V-8s, all with a 289 cubic inch displacement were optional.

The 200 hp Challenger V-8 retailed for $108 above the base engine with the 225 hp Challenger Special offered for an additional $58. Continued in the Mustang engine lineup was the Challenger High Performance V-8 with 271 hp. Included in its $327.92 (above the cost of the 200 hp V-8) price was the Special Handling Package and 6.95x14 dual red band sidewall nylon tires. If combined with the GT option the price was reduced to $276.34. Another option, whose price varied with the model on which it was ordered, was the Accent Group. When installed on either the Hardtop or Convertible its cost was $27.11. However, this price dropped to $13.90 for the 2+2. Any V-8 engined Mustang could be ordered with styled steel 14 inch wheels for $122.30. All Mustangs could be ordered with Kelsey-Hayes 9.5 inch cast iron front disc brakes for a reasonable $58. Available only for the Hardtop and Convertible Mustangs was a full width seat with a center arm-rest. A total of 14,905 Hardtops and 2,111 Convertibles were equipped with this 1965 1/2 option.

Another mid-year offering was the Interior Decor Group. Its listed price of $108.08 included padded sun visors, a woodgrain dash applique, deluxe wood grain steering wheel, red and white door courtesy lights and the five-dial dash cluster from the GT option. Hardtops with this feature were given a 65B body code. Respective body codes for similarly equipped 2+2 and Convertible Mustangs were 63 B and 76B. None of these were produced in large numbers. Output of 63B Mustangs was just 5,776. A total of 22,232 Hardtops were so equipped along with 5,338 Convertibles.

With the one-millionth Mustang produced on February 23, 1966, it was obvious that Americans were still head over heels in love with Ford's pony car. A model year output of 607,568 Mustangs underscored that fact!

Although none of the changes were drastic, the revisions to the Mustang's exterior for 1966 made it quite easy to identify the latest edition, whose rear panel "air scoop" now featured three horizontal bars. Horizontal bars also provided the background for the Mustang and its corral and all models carried the hood lip molding previously installed only on Mustangs with the GT option. The 1966 version of the GT package, retailing for $151.10, had a center grille spear linking the center ornament with the fog lights. No vertical grille bars were fitted. The GT package also included a special gas filter cap with stacked GT lettering in place of the standard cap, which was revised to allow for a larger Mustang logo. On early production models a new taillight arrangement with three separate lenses was installed but this feature was short lived with Ford reverting back to the original single lenses set up. Rounding out the new exterior features for 1966 were standard wheel covers with a five-spoke design in place of the concentric rings of earlier years and three new metallic colors (a total of 14 were offered), Dark Blue, Medium Palomino and Medium Sage Gold. All 1966 Mustangs were fitted with 14 inch wheels but those with six cylinder engines had four lugs instead of the five found in V-8 models.

Also common to all Mustangs for 1966 was the five-dial instrument panel that had previously been available only as part of the GT and Interior Decor Group options. However, the latter package now included a bevy of high-spirited mustangs embossed on the front and rear seat backs of Hardtop and Convertible models so equipped. The standard interior carried smooth front seat backs and seat inserts with a woven texture vinyl. On 2+2 models with the $93.45 Interior Decor Group only the front seats were decorated in this fashion. Also identifying Mustang with this option were door panel inserts with vertical instead of the standard horizontal pleats, red and white "Safety-Courtesy" lights built in to the lower door region and padded rear quarter panels. Matching the walnut appliques on the instrument panel and glove box door was the trim for the pistol grip door handles.

No changes were made in the Mustang's engine lineup for 1966, but for the first time Cruise-O-Matic was available with the 271 hp engine for $214.63. When ordered with the 200 cid 6, Cruise-O-Matic's price was $174.47. If ordered with either the 200 or 225 hp V-8s its price rose to $183.99.

Prices of the three Mustang models rose only moderately for the 1966 model year. The Hardtop and Convertible had respective base prices of $2,398.43 and $2,633.34. The 2+2 model was tagged at $2,587.89. Among the 70-plus options available for the Mustang was a new $184.65 AM radio with a Stereo-Sonic tape system. As in previous years, the most popular Mustang was the Hardtop version whose production totalled 499,751. Finishing second in this intramural competition was the Convertible with an output of 72,119 units. The final tally of 2+2 production was 35,798. The rarest of the 1966 Mustangs were the Convertibles with the front bench seat option, only 3,190 were assembled.

There were separate, attractive Mustang catalogues for 1964½, 1965 and 1966 (and revisions within model years). Excerpts from the 1966 edition appear on pages 9-15. The Mustang section from the "Total Performance" catalogue appears on pages 16-19. A 1965 Mustang ad appears on page 20, while a 1966 Mustang model car ad featuring a 1965 model (!) appears on page 21. The 1966 "Preview" mailer catalogue has been excerpted on page 22, the 1966 "Second Look" mailer catalogue on pages 23-24. A large color card was issued to celebrate the millionth Mustang and it is reproduced on page 25.

Rear seat luxury in the 2+2

Mustang Fastback 2+2

The Fastback 2+2 comes on bold with style you'd expect only from Europe and only at *very* high prices. But this one's a Mustang, with the kind of *low* Ford price that has made Mustang so popular.

Luxury with versatility comes in double handfuls. Silent-Flo Ventilation draws in a stream of fresh air with *all* windows closed. (Stale air, tobacco smoke exit out the louvers.) In the rear, the 2-passenger deep-foam seat folds down into a 35 x 41-in. platform, more than *tripling*

luggage space! The big 10-sq. ft. "skylight" window is tinted glass to cut sun glare.

A new standard 120-hp, 200-cu. in. Six is quick and strong . . . a quality thoroughbred, smooth as a jewel with its 7-main-bearing crankshaft. Thrifty, too, the Six is just one of many "savers" standard in Mustangs. Twice-a-Year Maintenance . . . self-adjusting brakes, aluminized muffler . . . plus all the other service savings pioneered by Ford. Any wonder that Mustangs are so easy to fall in love with?

2+2 cockpit: where spirited looks come alive!

Folding rear seat *triples* luggage space

2+2's Silent-Flo Ventilation louvers

Mustang Hardtop

When you look at Mustang's low price and the at all it includes as standard equipment, it's no wonder Mustang has come so far so fast. Take the Hardtop for instance. It's the lowest price of all three Mustangs. Yet that low price ta includes many luxury items, *standard on a* Mustangs, which come in other cars only a extra cost, or not at all.

Mustang's individually adjustable, deep-foam bucket seats

Trunk is surprisingly spacious, easy to load

See for yourself all that's standard in the Mustang Hardtop (and in the Convertible and 2+2 as well):

Individually Adjustable Deep-Foam Bucket Seats □ Padded Instrument Panel □ Full Wheel Covers □ Choice of 6 Color-Keyed All-Vinyl Interiors plus 2 Cloth-Vinyl Trims (Hardtop, 2+2) □ Color-Keyed Wall-to-Wall Carpeting.

Mustang's low price also includes these features which often cost extra in other cars:

Sports Steering Wheel with Bright-Metal Horn Arms □ Cigarette Lighter □ 2 Automatic Courtesy Lights □ Glove Box Light □ Floor Shift 3-Speed Manual Transmission.

Mustang's low price also includes these features as standard equipment:

120-hp 6-Cylinder Engine □ Heater-Defroster* □ Front Seat Belts* □ Front Arm Rests □ Electric Windshield Wipers □ Safety-Yoke Door Latches □ Curved Side Glass □ Wrap-Around Front Bumper □ Bumper Guards Front and Rear □ Alternator □ "Sta-Ful" Battery □ Ford's Famous Twice-a-Year Maintenance Features (back cover).

*See "Prices" on back cover

Mustang Convertible

What kind of convertible will your Mustang be—family fun-in-the-sun car . . . full-fledged sports soft-top or luxury convertible? Mustang Convertible standard equipment gives you a great head start.

A 5-ply, vinyl-bonded top (in color choice of black, white or tan) with big "zip-out" window for straight-through ventilation. A color-keyed, stretch-taut boot to stow the top neat and trim. Deep-foam bucket seats that adjust individually. Choice of six leather-soft, all-vinyl interiors. Full carpeting. Courtesy lighting. A slick 3-speed floor shift. A quick, strong 120-hp, 200-cu. in. Six has the quality and smoothness of a 7-main-bearing crankshaft. Plus all the other standard equipment listed on page 6!

Now the fun begins with Mustang options. New full-width front seat* with folding center arm rest (in four all-vinyl trim choices). New Interior Decor Group (next pages). New GT Equipment Group (pages 14-15). T-bar Cruise-O-Matic or 4-speed manual transmissions. Challenger V-8's of 200, 225, 271 hp. Rally Pac. Power top. Front disc brakes. Tonneau cover. Power steering. Ford Air Conditioner. Power brakes. And so many, many more.

However you design your Mustang, you can depend on the *versatility* that is as much a part of Mustang as the driving fun. From the twice-daily trip to school to a gala debut at the country club, Mustangs go *everywhere* . . . do *everything!*

*In Hardtop, Convertible

Six all-vinyl trim choices with the look and feel of leather

Power top is one of over 70 options

Tonneau cover adds true sports-car flair

Equipment Group

Anybody who goes for performance will go for the new Mustang GT Equipment Group. Ten separate items—and what a great performance package it all adds up to!

☐ Hot 225-hp Challenger Special V-8 (10 to 1 comp. ratio, 4-barrel carb.). ☐ *Fully* synchronized 3-speed manual floor shift. ☐ Dual straight-through exhaust system with flared, chrome tail-pipe extensions.

And, in addition you get: ☐ Mustang's Special Handling Package (heavy-duty suspension, 22 to 1 overall steering ratio. ☐ Fade-resisting front disc brakes. ☐ A pair of 4-inch fog lamps nestled in the grille.

The GT Equipment Group also includes: ☐ Five-dial instrument cluster (fuel, temperature, speedometer, oil pressure, amperes) set in a background of black leather-grained vinyl. ☐ Handsome "GT" fender badges placed just aft of each front wheel cutout. ☐ Bright-metal hood accent molding. ☐ And running front to rear along the lower body is the triple stripe that Ford's GT racing car carries in European competition!

If you'd like to make some modifications to the basic GT Equipment Group (say move up to the 271-hp Challenger High Performance V-8 and 4-speed stick shift), go right ahead. Or if you'd prefer some additions (like Rally Pac, red band or white sidewall tires, racing mirrors, styled steel wheels), be our guest. These are separate Mustang options—and there are many more besides—which will fit perfectly with the GT Equipment Group.

See what kind of a GT Mustang *you* can dream up for your choice of the Mustang Hardtop, Convertible or Fastback 2+2!

*Available also as separate option

†Separate option, not included in GT Group

4-Inch Fog Lamps

GT Instrument Cluster

4-Speed Stick Shift‡   Fender Badge   Handling Package*

Rally Pac†

Mustang Interior Decor Group

Steering wheel, instrument panel have rich, woodlike finish

Coming up with a super-luxurious interior for Mustang is no small order. But see for yourself how Ford stylists have created an interior of *special* Mustang elegance.

There's a custom-tailored look to the leather-soft vinyl seat trim (with Mustang duo-tone embossing) and pleated door panels. Rich, simulated walnut paneling enhances the five-dial instrument cluster, glove box door and console* between the seats.

Wood-grained deluxe steering wheel† looks like select walnut, has sporty perforated metal spokes. Horn buttons are at outer ends of the spokes.

Sun visors are safety-padded and color-keyed. Integral arm rests blend smoothly into each door panel. Door hardware is unique. There is a dual-lens light at the lower edge of each door. It shines a red warning beam to the rear and a clear "courtesy" beam into the car when either door is opened.

Floor pedals are trimmed in bright metal. Molded carpeting stretches luxuriously wall to wall and trims front cowl panels.

Available in your choice of seven colors, the Interior Decor Group is Mustang at its most elegant.

*Optional †Available also as separate option

Door panels have integral arm rests, safety-courtesy lights

MUSTANG

A Marvel of Motion

The Mustang by the Ford Division of Ford Motor Company is the newest car on the American Road. Its evolution is from the Ford Styling Department's experimental "X-cars" — the Mustang I and the Mustang II — sporty, personal cars directed to the "fun-to-drive" market. The enthusiastic public reaction to the forerunners of the production Mustang indicated that a substantial number of buyers were looking for a type of American passenger car that was not available to the average buyer, so the experimental "X-cars" were developed further to become practical production models. Also, as intended, the Mustang displays much Thunderbird ancestry that was incorporated because of the still existent public interest in the two-passenger T'Bird as offered in 1957.

In the comparison of selected data of the 1957 Thunderbird and the Mustang, it is shown that the Mustang has a longer wheelbase, is longer overall, lower, has the same wide tread, and it is over 400 pounds lighter. Obviously, the Mustang is a more agile car than the '57 T'Bird and, in addition, it will accommodate four passengers instead of just two because of the two-plus two seating arrangement made possible by better space utilization.

In the performance and economy area, the Mustang equipped with the optional 289-cubic-inch V-8 and a 4-speed manual transmission will out accelerate a 1957 T'Bird by 73 feet in ten seconds from a standing start — *the Thunderbird had a 292-cubic-inch engine and used premium fuel.* In an economy test, the Mustang averaged 16.6 miles per gallon; while the Thunderbird averaged 13.7 miles per gallon, or about three miles less than Mustang.

Although new in concept, the Mustang hardtop or convertible will provide a high degree of reliability and durability due to the blending of established powertrain and chassis components. These components have been proven by engineering tests, customer usage, and in every type of competitive event on the road or track.

A unique design feature of the Mustang is its *platform chassis construction.* Ford is the first manufacturer to employ this design on an American-made car. Until now, it has been available only on a few of the higher priced European sports cars.

The platform provides the basic foundation of the car. It carries the body, encloses the engine, and provides attaching points for the various chassis components.

The platform consists of box-section front and rear side rails tied in securely to heavy boxed-in rocker panels. Heavy gage crossmembers connect these basic platform components to form a ladder type framing beneath the car. The full-depth, full-length tunnel in the floor pan adds a "backbone" down the center of the structure to provide maximum rigidity.

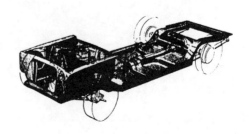

MUSTANG HIGH-PERFORMANCE

For those who want the ultimate in power and performance, Mustang can be equipped with the 289-cubic-inch high-performance V-8*. This engine is for the true driving enthusiast who wants sports car performance to complement Mustang's sports car styling—the type of performance that must be experienced behind the wheel to be appreciated. The "289" high-performance engine features solid valve lifters, header-type exhaust system, high-lift camshaft, and a low-restriction air cleaner for the special 4-venturi carburetor. This engine is rated at 271 horsepower, which provides Mustang with the performance characteristics of a top contender at rallies, gymkhanas, and other sports events. *A Mustang test car equipped with the "289" high-performance engine and a 4-speed manual transmission traveled 621 feet in ten seconds from a standing start.*

MUSTANG PERFORMANCE AND ECONOMY

To make Mustang one of the top performing cars on the road, and for those who desire reserve power and the economy of regular fuel, the 210 horsepower 289-cubic-inch V-8 is offered. The Ford constant-mesh 3-speed manual transmission is standard with this engine, and the 4-speed manual or the Cruise-O-Matic are optional. *A Mustang test car equipped with the regular "289" engine and a 4-speed manual transmission traveled 584 feet in ten seconds from a standing start.*

For a lively personal car with smooth, quiet V-8 power, plus economy of operation, the buyer may choose the 260-cubic-inch V-8. This engine is rated at 164 horsepower, and the Ford 3-speed constant-mesh transmission is standard. Cruise-O-Matic is optional. *A Mustang test car equipped with this engine traveled 524 feet in ten seconds from a standing start.*

MUSTANG ECONOMY

The Mustang 170-cubic-inch Six is the standard equipment engine. With a rating of 101 horsepower, the "170" provides Mustang with performance characteristics that are more than adequate for city traffic plus all-day turnpike cruising. With the standard 3-speed manual transmission, the "170" Mustang is the most economical means of driving America's newest car. The 4-speed manual transmission or the Cruise-O-Matic are optional. *A Mustang test car equipped with the "170" engine traveled 440 feet in ten seconds from a standing start.*

MUSTANG SPECIAL HANDLING

The Special Handling Package is available for those who desire quicker, more precise handling and increased roadability. Included in the package are increased rate front and rear springs, an increased diameter front stabilizer bar, 14-inch tires and wheels with 5-inch rims, and a faster steering gear that results in a 22:1 overall steering ratio. *When equipped with the "289" high performance engine, all items of the Special Handling Package, with the exception of the 22:1 steering ratio, are included.*

POWER TEAM SELECTION CHART

ENGINES	TRANSMISSIONS			REAR AXLE RATIOS		
	3-Speed Manual	4-Speed Manual	Cruise-O-Matic	3-Speed Manual	4-Speed Manual	Cruise-O-Matic
"170" Six—Std.	Std.	Opt.	Opt.	3.50	3.50	3.50
"260" V-8—Opt.	Std.	N/A	Opt.	3.00	N/A	3.00
"289" V-8—Opt.	N/A	Opt.	Opt.	N/A	3.00	3.00
**"289" V-8—Opt. Hi-Performance	N/A	Opt.	N/A	N/A	3.89 4.11	N/A

Available after June 1, 1964

The Mustang I is a development of Ford Motor Company engineers and stylists — men who have an intense interest in modern sports cars and who have particular ideas of what the American sports car should possess in performance characteristics and functional design.

Beneath the aluminum skin of the Mustang are engineering and styling innovations that are conceivable for Ford cars of the near future. The *space frame* is a tubular steel frame that is reinforced by the aluminum sheet metal body skin . . . *the 60-degree V-4 engine — transaxle* with a three-mount system that supports the entire unit . . . *the combined-unit coil springs and shock absorbers* that can be adjusted to vary the riding height up to 1.25 inches . . . *the suspension system with tubular arms* that are fully stressed to minimize weight . . . *the adjustable accelerator, brake, and clutch pedals* that can be moved fore and aft to a distance of four inches to permit the seat structure to be fixed to the body for greater structural rigidity and safety . . . the *adjustable steering column* that features a three-inch fore and aft adjustment for superior driving comfort . . . the *brakes with dual master hydraulic cylinders* for greater safety . . . and the *cast magnesium wheels* to minimize the unsprung weight.

The Mustang II, while inspired by the original Mustang, is considerably larger and features more conventional chassis and drive line components. It is best described as a sporty, personal vehicle that is designed for the motoring enthusiast who wants a "fun-to-drive" car.

The Mustang II is 186.6 inches long on a 108 inch wheelbase. Overall width is 68.2 inches, overall height 48.4 inches. Outstanding performance is supplied by a 289 cubic-inch V-8 engine.

The interior features thin-shell bucket seats front and rear. The seat backs in the coved rear compartment are integrated with the rear deck, and a console between the front seats sweeps up to merge with the instrument panel.

Also featured is a detachable hardtop roof, a refinement of the popular Thunderbird design.

MUSTANG SPECIFICATIONS

BODY SPECIFICATIONS

GENERAL	HARDTOP	CONVERTIBLE
Wheelbase	108.0	108.0
Tread—Front	55.4 (56.0)	55.4 (56.0)
—Rear	56.0	56.0
Height—Overall	51.1	51.0
Width—Overall	68.2	68.2
Length—Overall	181.6	181.6
LUGGAGE CAPACITY		
Usable Luggage Capacity	8.9 cu. ft.	7.0 cu. ft.
GLASS AREA		
Side Glass Exposed Surface Area	1038.4 sq. in.	1038.4 sq. in.
Windshield Exposed Surface Area	1022.4 sq. in.	1072.4 sq. in.
Backlight Exposed Surface Area	816.2 sq. in.	826.0 sq. in.
Total Glass Exposed Surface Area	2927.0 sq. in.	2936.8 sq. in.

( ) V-8 MODELS
NOTE: All dimensions are in inches unless otherwise noted.

ENGINE SPECIFICATIONS

	170 SIX	260 V-8	289 V-8	289 HP V-8
TYPE	6-CYL. IN-LINE OHV	90° V OHV		
BORE AND STROKE—IN.	3.50 x 2.94	3.80 x 2.87	4.00 x 2.87	
COMPRESSION RATIO	8.7:1	8.8:1	9.0:1	10.5:1
BRAKE HORSEPOWER @ RPM	101 @ 4400	164 @ 4400	210 @ 4400	271 @ 6000
MAXIMUM TORQUE— LBS.-FT. @ RPM	156 @ 2400	258 @ 2200	300 @ 2400	312 @ 3400
VALVE LIFTERS	HYDRAULIC			SOLID
CARBURETOR	1-V	2-V	4-V	
FUEL	REGULAR			PREMIUM

TRANSMISSION GEAR RATIOS

	FIRST	SECOND	THIRD	FOURTH	REVERSE
CONVENTIONAL THREE-SPEED MANUAL—SIX-CYL.	3.29:1	1.83:1	1.00:1	—	4.46:1
CONSTANT-MESH, THREE-SPEED MANUAL	2.79:1	1.70:1	1.00:1	—	2.87:1
FOUR-SPEED MANUAL—SIX-CYL.	3.16:1	2.21:1	1.41:1	1.00:1	3.35:1
CRUISE-O-MATIC	2.46:1	1.46:1	1.00:1	—	2.20:1
FOUR-SPEED MANUAL—289 V-8	2.78:1	1.93:1	1.36:1	1.00:1	2.78:1
FOUR-SPEED MANUAL—High Performance-289 V-8	2.32:1	1.69:1	1.29:1	1.00:1	2.32:1

CLUTCH SPECIFICATIONS

	170 SIX	260 V-8	289 V-8	289 HI-PERF.
TYPE	SINGLE DRY PLATE, CUSHION DISC			
PILOT BEARING	OIL-IMPREGNATED BRONZE			
THROW-OUT BEARING	PRE-LUBRICATED, SEALED, BALL-TYPE			
FACE DIAMETER	8.5″	10.0″	10.4″	10.4″
TOTAL FRICTIONAL AREA	68.1 SQ. IN.	85.1 SQ. IN.	103.7 SQ. IN.	103.7 SQ. IN.

WHEEL SPECIFICATIONS

	6-CYL. MODELS	V-8 MODELS
TYPE	STAMPED STEEL VENTILATED DISC WITH SAFETY TYPE RIMS	
NUMBER OF STUDS	4	5
DIAMETER AND RIM SIZE (IN.) STANDARD	13 X 4.5	13 X 4.5
OPTIONAL	14 X 4.5	14 X 5

DRIVE SHAFT AND UNIVERSAL JOINTS

DRIVE TYPE	HOTCHKISS
DRIVE SHAFT	SINGLE PIECE, HOLLOW TUBE
UNIVERSAL JOINTS	CROSS AND YOKE, NEEDLE BEARING
LUBRICATION INTERVAL	36,000 MILES

TIRE SPECIFICATIONS

	6.50 X 13 4 PR	7.00 X 13 4 PR	6.50 X 14 4 PR	5.60/5.90 X 15
6-CYLINDER MODELS	STD.	—	OPT.	—
8-CYLINDER MODELS	STD.	OPT.*	OPT.	—
8-CYLINDER MODELS WITH SPECIAL HANDLING PACKAGE	—	—	STD.	OPT.

*Standard with air conditioning.
NOTE: All 13- and 14-inch tires are available in WSW.

REAR AXLE SPECIFICATIONS

	SIX-CYLINDER MODELS	V-8 MODELS
TYPE	HYPOID, SEMIFLOATING	
HOUSING	MALLEABLE IRON, INTEGRAL CARRIER	PRESSED-STEEL, REMOVABLE CARRIER
DRIVE TYPE	HOTCHKISS	
DIFFERENTIAL	DEEP-OFFSET, HYPOID	
AXLE SHAFTS	INDUCTION-HARDENED STEEL FORGINGS	
WHEEL BEARINGS	DOUBLE-SEALED, BALL-TYPE PERMANENTLY LUBRICATED	

BRAKE SPECIFICATIONS

	6-CYL.	8-CYL.
BRAKE DRUM DIAMETER	9″	10″
LINING MATERIAL	MOLDED ASBESTOS	
LINING ATTACHMENT	RIVETED	
TOTAL LINING AREA—GROSS (SQ. IN.)	131.0	154.2

SUSPENSION SPECIFICATIONS

FRONT

TYPE	INDEPENDENT WITH BALL JOINTS
SPRINGS	4″ ID HELICAL COIL, RUBBER INSULATED
SHOCK ABSORBERS	HYDRAULIC, TELESCOPIC, VERTICAL-MOUNT
STABILIZER	LINK-TYPE, RUBBER-BUSHED
STEERING KNUCKLE	INTEGRAL SPINDLE AND SPINDLE SUPPORT
WHEEL BEARINGS	OPPOSED TAPERED ROLLER

REAR

TYPE	VARIABLE RATE, LONGITUDINAL SEMIELLIPTIC LEAF SPRINGS WITH RUBBER-BUSHED HANGERS
NUMBER OF LEAVES	4
LEAF LENGTH AND WIDTH	53″ X 2.5″
SPRING SHACKLES	COMPRESSION-TYPE, RUBBER-BUSHED
SHOCK ABSORBERS	HYDRAULIC, TELESCOPIC, ANGLE MOUNT

STEERING SPECIFICATIONS

LINKAGE .... PARALLELOGRAM WITH CROSS LINK AND IDLER ARM
GEAR-TYPE .... MAGIC-CIRCLE RECIRCULATING BALL
OVERALL STEERING RATIO
    MANUAL .... 27 TO 1
    POWER AND HANDLING PACKAGE .... 22 TO 1
STEERING WHEEL
    DIAMETER .... 16 INCHES

STEERING WHEEL TURNS
(LOCK-TO-LOCK)
    MANUAL 4½
    POWER AND HANDLING PACKAGE 3½
TURNING DIAMETER
    (CURB-TO-CURB) .... 38.0 FEET

Put Cobra sting in your Mustang 289 block

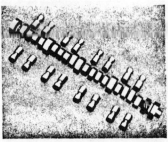

Cobra Two 4-V Induction Kit: Use this kit to achieve greater performance without drastic modification of your 289 mill. Kit includes two 4-barrel carburetors, two air cleaners, special cast aluminum intake manifold. Helps develop maximum speed and horsepower in engines modified for hot competition. Part #C4OZ-6B068-E . . . $245.00*

Cobra Distributor Kit: This high-performance kit consists of heavy-duty distributor and leads. Features dual points, centrifugal spark advance. Use the kit to give your engine the ignition-advance performance characteristics you want for high RPM action. Part #C4DZ-12050-A . . . $49.80*

Cobra Cam Kit: This kit has been specially engineered with correct tolerances for 260 or 289 blocks. Consists of finely machined camshaft and 16 tappets, is same type used in winning Cobras. Part #C4OZ-6A257-A . . . $75.10*

*Manufacturer's suggested retail price. Installation, state and local taxes, if any, are extra.

PRODUCTS OF *Ford*

Customize your Mustang with these GT parts: Your Ford Dealer has a wealth of great GT equipment waiting for you. GT stripe, simulated wood-grained steering wheel, special GT grille with built-in fog lamps, dual exhaust system with chrome "trumpet" extensions; backup lights. See your Ford Dealer for prices and full details.

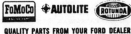

QUALITY PARTS FROM YOUR FORD DEALER

RIDE WALT DISNEY'S MAGIC SKYWAY AT THE FORD MOTOR COMPANY PAVILION, NEW YORK WORLD'S FAIR

Just in time for Christmas, and only at your Ford Dealer's

Motorized
MUSTANG GT

SPECIALLY PRICED AT ONLY
$4.95

Everyone with young ideas likes Mustang. That's why Mustang is the most successful new car ever introduced. Mustang is a car built for fun! And now there's Mustang fun for fans too young to drive...the exciting 1966 Motorized Mustang GT!

This brilliant Poppy Red Motorized Mustang GT is the perfect holiday gift for youngsters! It captures all the flavor of its big brother; it's a perfectly-detailed operating model of a 1966 Mustang GT Hardtop.

The Motorized Mustang GT is a big 16 inches long! Manufactured exclusively for Ford Dealers, it's battery operated, with a motor that

propels it forwards and backwards, has working headlights and taillights—and even the batteries are included. The front wheels are fully adjustable for steering and there's a simulated Mustang V-8 engine under the hood!

Like the real Mustang, the Motorized Mustang GT is strong, sturdy, and built to last. For racing buffs a conversion kit (gasoline engine and slicks) and remote control throttle may also be ordered.

So stop in at your Ford Dealer's, pick up a Motorized Mustang GT for the children...and take a look at its big brother. Make this a *real* holiday with the Motorized Mustang GT for the young set and a full-size Mustang for yourself!

See your Ford Dealer...test drive a Mustang!

America's Favorite Fun Car

MUSTANG
MUSTANG
MUSTANG

The ultimate Total Performance car (below), the fabulous Ford GT. And here are the cars it inspired, the three Mustang GT's for '66! The Mustang GT equipment includes: low-restriction trumpet exhausts, 3-speed floor shift, fade-resistant front disc brakes, a pair of 4-inch fog lamps, Special Handling Package, exclusive GT stripe (just like the Ford GT) and special GT insignia. Optional are 225-hp or 271-hp V-8, 4-speed gearbox or Cruise-O-Matic Drive.

TAKE A SECOND LOOK

Your second look at Mustang for '66 will reveal in greater detail: the most successful new car ever introduced.

You probably noticed the thoughtfully planned styling refinements in this year's three Mustangs — Hardtop, Convertible and Fastback 2 + 2. An eye-catching new grille, crisply styled side scoops and new hood lip molding — these are a few of the touches that add to Mustang's rakish, sporty air.

But did you look under Mustang's hood? You should — that's where the action is! A 200-cu. in., 120-hp Six is standard, or optional power that charges all the way up to a 289-cu. in., 271-hp Cobra V-8 plus 200- and 225-hp engines in between . . . a total of eleven power teams.

Personalized music is all but unlimited if you select Mustang's AM Radio/Stereo-sonic Tape System. This unique option surrounds you with over 70 minutes of uninterrupted music, prerecorded on easy-to-insert tape cartridges.

One of the best places to look at Mustang is from the driver's seat (a deep-comfort bucket seat). From this position you can survey much of what makes Mustang so regal: plus wall-to-wall carpeting, handy floor-mounted stick shift, a richly padded instrument panel and sun visors and vinyl upholstery. All of this is standard Mustang. And so are padded front arm rests, a fresh air heater, automatic courtesy lighting, backup lights, and seat belts front and rear.

Mustang's option list includes over 70 items. Among the features you'll find are power brakes, power steering, front disc brakes, 4-speed stick shift or Cruise-O-Matic, and tinted glass all-around or for windshield only. For still more sport and luxury, you can choose the GT Equipment and Interior Decor Groups for '66.

Had enough? Not until you slide behind the wheel of one of this year's spirited Mustangs and put it through its paces. That's when Mustang will really come alive for you!

Cruise-O-Matic transmission

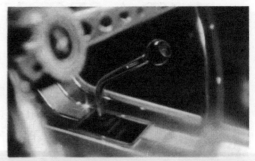

Optional 4-speed stick shift

GT insignia

Eleven power team choices

Optional AM Radio/Stereo-sonic Tape System

Interior Decor Group includes deluxe bucket seats, wood-grained accents, and embossed trim

25

1967-1968

After three years of existence when it was faced with only token resistance from Barracuda and Marlin, the Mustang found itself challenged not only by a sharply redesigned Barracuda and Chevrolet's new Camaro, but, at the upper price level of its class, by Mercury's Cougar. Ford responded with a substantially revamped Mustang, with an even greater choice of options and, for the first time, a 390 cid V-8 engine. But with the pony car field becoming so crowded, it was almost inevitable that Mustang production would drop substantially. Nonetheless, model year output was a respectable 472,121.

With new sheet metal below the beltline, the Mustang retained the basic exterior form of earlier years but in subtle ways assumed a more mature stance. Contributing to this evolution was an additional two inches of overall length (all of which was found forward of the headlights) and an increase of two inches in its overall width. With its wheelbase unchanged at 108 inches, the Mustang now measured 183.6 inches from bumper to bumper with a width of 70.9 inches. Both the Hardtop and Convertible measured 51.6 inches in height. The 2+2's height increased slightly to 51.8 inches from 51.6 inches. However, the 2+2 body was sleeker with its roofline flowing smoothly into the rear deck. A new tapered form for the twelve C-pillar louvers of the flow-through ventilation system blended nicely into this new design.

While all three body styles had more concave rear panels, the rear deck line of the 2+2 was heightened to encompass Mustang lettering spaced across the deck lid.

Among the detail changes made in the Mustang's side trim was a new two-piece simulated rear fender grille and revised engine displacement labels. Those Mustangs with the base engine bore the standard Mustang emblem. V-8 Mustangs had either 289 or 390 numbers added to the top of the tri-color bar.

The addition of the 320 hp, 390 cubic inch Thunderbird Special V-8 to the Mustang's engine lineup enabled a customer to select from thirteen engine-transmission combinations. This engine's maximum horsepower was reached at 4800 rpm and its peak torque was an impressive 427 lb-ft at 3200 rpm. A single four-barrel carburetor was fitted and a 10.5:1 compression ratio was specified. Cruise-O-Matic, which was now of the SelectShift variety, was available with any of the Mustang's five engines.

Changes to the Mustang's suspension were intended to both cope with the added weight of the 390 engine (which was priced at $158.08) and provide a smoother, quieter ride. Revised front suspension geometry resulted in a higher front roll center which helped keep the outside wheel perpendicular to the road. Rubber bushings were used to eliminate all metal-to-metal contacts between all suspension components. In place of the metal bearings used previously in the front suspension ball-joint sockets was a polyethylene filling. The Mustang's rear suspension consisted, as it had in previous years, of leaf springs with asymmetrically positioned shock absorbers.

Seasoned Mustang watchers were quick to note that the 2+2's standard rear seat was stationary (the fold down version was now available as the Sport Deck option) and that the convertible top could be equipped with a neat glass window which folded along a horizontal hinge when the top was lowered. Common to all models was a new dash dominated by two large circular dials on each side of the steering column. The 0-120 mph speedometer was positioned on the left with its counterpart housing gauges for oil pressure and alternator. Interspersed above these instruments were smaller versions for the fuel level, engine temperature and, when ordered, an electric clock. When the 0-6000 tachometer was installed it assumed the location of the oil pressure-alternator cluster. Warning lights for these functions were also provided.

Among the Mustang's options being offered for the first time were a tilt-swing steering column with nine different positions. When the engine was turned off, the transmission placed in park and the driver's door opened, the wheel could be swung 45 degree to the car's center. Also debuting as 1967 options were power front disc brakes and Fingertip Speed Control which had a range from 20 to 80 mph.

The GT option, retailing for $205.05 was continued and for 1967 included Wide Oval Firestone F70-14 tires, power front disc brakes and a special handling package with higher rate springs and shocks plus a larger front stabilizer bar. With either the Cobra or Thunderbird Special V-8 a dual exhaust system with chromed quad outlets was installed. The rocker panel molding included in this package was smooth instead of ribbed and the lower body striping carried GTA lettering for Mustangs with Cruise-O-Matic or GT if a manual transmission was installed. Mustangs with the GT package and either the 271 hp or 320 hp engines could be equipped with the $388.53 Competition Handling Package. This feature included Koni adjustable shocks, 16:1 manual steering, a 3.21:1 limited slip rear axle, disc brakes and even stiffer springs.

Once again the Hardtop version, priced at $2,482.46, was the most popular Mustang, with a total output of 356,271. The 2+2 Fastback listing for $2,613.17 had a production run of 71,042 cars. The Convertible, which at $2,719.14 was the most expensive Mustang, was also the Mustang seen the least, only 44,800 were completed during the model year.

The following year, 1968, was a year of Mustang design transition. A bigger and heavier model was ready for a 1969 debut but the explosive popularity of the muscle cars mandated the immediate availability of even larger and more powerful engine options for the Mustang. Ford wasn't ignoring the Mustang's basic market strength but at the same time it was going to make certain that Mustang owners would be able to challenge the 400+ cubic inch supercars on their own turf.

When the model year began in September, 1967, a total of twelve engine-transmission combinations were available for the Mustang. The basic 200 cid, 115 hp six was offered with either a three-speed manual or Cruise-O-Matic. The last of the 289 cid V-8s for the Mustang, a 195 hp version with an 8.7:1 compression ratio, hydraulic lifters and a single two-barrel Autolite carburetor would be replaced later in the season by a 302 cid V-8 rated at 220 hp. Both engines were available with either three- or four-speed manual gearboxes plus Cruise-O-Matic. A second version of Ford's 302 cid V-8 was part of the Mustang's original engine lineup. The Challenger Special V-8, available with the same trio of gearboxes, offered a reasonable 230 hp and featured a 10.0:1 compression ratio and a four-barrel Autolite carburetor. Coming aboard the Mustang engine option list late in 1967 was the 302 cid, High Performance V-8. This was the fabled tunnelport 302 which Ford advised was available on special order only and, with an 11.0:1 compression ratio and a single Holley four-barrel carburetor, was rated at 345 hp. The addition of such dealer-installed options as domed pistons and dual Holley four-barrel carburetors moved its maximum horsepower into the 400 range.

More familiar to most Mustang enthusiasts was the 390 cid Thunderbird Special V-8 whose 325 hp could be harnessed to either Cruise-O-Matic or a four-speed manual transmission. More exciting however was the 1968½ 427 cid Cobra Jet which was installed in a mere handful of Mustangs. Priced at $622.97 above the price of the 289 Challenger V-8 (which was tagged at $105.63 above the base six cylinder engine) it carried a maximum rating of 390 hp. Acquisition of this engine also required ordering of the GT group option.

The Mustang's "something for everybody" sales philosophy had received even more credence in November 1967, when a 280 hp, two-barrel carburetor 390 cid V-8 plus the 428 cid Cobra Jet V-8 were tacked on to its option list. The latter engine had conservative ratings of 335 hp at 5400 rpm and 440 lb-ft at 3400 rpm. Included in its $420.96 price was a cold air hood for its single Holley 735 cfm four-barrel and Goodyear Polyglas wide oval, F70x14 tires on 6-inch rims. Either four-speed manual or Cruise-O-Matic transmissions were available.

Measured against this dazzling array of engine choices the Mustang's styling changes were modest. A new grille emblem with a thinner corral for the galloping mustang was backdropped by a simple mesh screen and a grille within a grille design was created by the addition of an inner trim ring. A few early 1968 models had the louvered hood installed as standard equipment. However, the vast majority of Mustangs had a smooth hood. Removed for 1968 was the Ford lettering across the front hood edge. All models carried the front side lights and rear reflectors as mandated by the federal government. The dual rear fender scoops of 1967 were replaced by a less pretentious but still artificial one-piece unit.

Primary interior changes included a change in direction for the seat pleats, which now ran lengthwise, and a standard energy-absorbing steering column with a two-spoke steering wheel. The instrument panel arrangement was unaltered except for two minor revisions. The shape of the brake warning light panel and wiper control bar were now arrow-shaped instead of rectangular and the oil pressure gauge was now placed where the gas level indicator had previously been located. The final portion of this reshuffle located the alternator and fuel level dials in the large circular gauge adjacent to the speedometer.

Among the Mustang's options available for the first time was an AM/FM stereo radio ($61) and, for the Hardtop and 2+2, a new window defogger. The GT option, priced at $147 and available only for Mustangs with V-8s above the 289 cid Challenger V-8, continued to feature such components as fog lamps, stiffer suspension and wide oval tires. Revised for 1969 was its side striping which now outlined the side concave. The GT front fender plaque was larger and special slotted wheels with stacked GT letters in the center hub were included in the package.

With competition more intense than ever, Ford made certain that if a market segment opened up, a Mustang would be ready to fill it. Late in 1967 two Mustangs identified as Mustang Sprints were offered. The 6-cylinder version was equipped with such features as GT striping, pop-open gas cap and special wheel covers. The V-8 version was available with GT fog lamps, styled steel wheels and wide-oval tires. Limited to the California market was the Mustang GT/CS (California Special), identified by its Lucas rectangular fog lamps, blacked-out grille, louvered hood with turnscrew locks, rear deck spoiler and wide taillights borrowed from the 1965 Thunderbird. In addition, mid-body striping was applied which ran from the front fender to a non-functional pod-like rear fender air scoop. Yet another variation, the Mustang E, a 2+2 fastback with an automatic transmission, 155 hp, 250 cid six cylinder engine and a 2.33:1 rear axle came to market in November, 1967.

The Mustang's 1968 model year production totalled 317,148 units and once again the Hardtop, base priced at $2,602, was the public's number one choice. A total of 249,447 were assembled. Far behind was the 2+2 with a 42,325 production run and the Convertible, of which only 25,376 were manufactured. Beginning prices of these two latter models were $2,712 and $2,745 respectively.

There were attractive Mustang catalogues for 1967 and 1968, although the format was changed from horizontal to vertical for the latter year. Due to their popularity, Mustangs continued to be included in most of the full-line Ford brochures. The Mustang section from the comprehensive 1967 "Ford Buyer's Digest" is reproduced here (see pages 28-31), as well as excerpts from the Mustang catalogue (see pages 32 and 38-39). The Mustang spread from the full-line "Second Look" mailer catalogue appears on pages 36-37 and three magazine ads are reproduced on pages 33-35, including one for the special Sprint model. The 1968 literature included features the rare GT/CS folder (see pages 42-44). A two panel ad on the special 1968 Sprint model appears on pages 40-41 and a flyer on the rare "Branded Mustangs" dealer option appears on page 45.

Buyer's Digest
OF NEW CAR FACTS FOR 1967

The Original Ford Book for Car Buyers Who Want
All the Facts Before Making a Purchasing Decision

9TH YEAR

MUSTANG

HARDTOP
AND CONVERTIBLE

Mustang—bred first to be first—presents three new models for 1967, including the new Fastback 2+2 with the full sloping roof, on the next page. All three models have a sporty new body, a longer, wider look, and a wider tread for better road grip. But the flavor and feel—the things that made Mustang the most popular new car ever introduced—these are as Mustangy as ever.

Mustang's standard equipment is even *more* all-inclusive than before. In addition to bucket front seats, carpeting, and all-vinyl upholstery, Mustang now has all the standard Ford Motor Company Lifeguard-Design Safety Features (page 18) . . . and these include the new dual brake system with separate lines and a dual master cylinder for the front and rear brakes. Mustang also features Ford Motor Company's "3-Point Warranty Plan" with power train, suspension and steering components warranted for five years or 50,000 miles (page 47). V-8 engine options are now available up to 320 hp. SelectShift Cruise-O-Matic, which offers both manual and automatic shifting, is another new Mustang option. Others are shown on pages 17 and 60. Optional choices are so numerous that you can almost literally design your own Mustang.

Ford's Twice-a-Year Maintenance features are still very much a part of Mustang. That means three years or 36,000 miles between major lube jobs, an alternator and a long-life battery, and numerous other advantages which save you money and trouble, add to Mustang fun and liveliness.

Standard Equipment Highlights

200-cu. in., 120-hp Six Engine ▪ 3-Speed Synchro-Smooth Manual Transmission with Floor-Mounted Shift Lever ▪ Ford Motor Company Lifeguard-Design Safety Features such as Two-Speed Parallel-Action Electric Windshield Wipers and Washer, Backup Lights and many more (see page 18) ▪ Outside Rearview Mirror ▪ Suspended Foot Pedals ▪ Automatic Choke ▪ Long-Life Sta-Ful Battery ▪ Alternator ▪ Self-Adjusting Brakes and Valves ▪ 6000-Mile or 6-Month Oil Filter ▪ 36,000-Mile or 2-Year Coolant-Antifreeze ▪ Fully Aluminized Muffler ▪ Galvanized Main Underbody Members ▪ Reversible Ignition, Door and Trunk Keys ▪ Bright-Metal Windshield and Rear Window Moldings ▪ Curved Glass Side Windows ▪ Super Diamond Lustre Enamel ▪ Automatic Courtesy Lighting ▪ Front Bucket Seats ▪ Rocker Panel Moldings (2+2) ▪ Sunburst Wheel Covers (2+2) ▪ Color-Keyed Steering Wheel with Sports Horn Bars ▪ Color-Keyed Carpeting, Front and Rear ▪ Choice of Seven All-Vinyl Upholsteries and 16 Exterior Color Choices—see Upholstery and Color pages at back of book ▪ 5-Ply Vinyl Convertible Top, Manually Operated, in White or Black ▪ Fresh Air Heater-Defroster

Basic Specifications

Length—183.6″ ▪ Width—70.9″ ▪ Height—51.6″ ▪ Wheelbase—108″ ▪ Curb Weight (approx.)—Hardtop 2696 lb.; Convertible 2856 lb.; 2+2 2723 lb. ▪ Trunk Luggage Volume—Hardtop 9.2 cu. ft.; Convertible 7.7 cu. ft.; 2+2 5.1 cu. ft.

Optional Mustang Engines and Transmissions

Four optional V-8's: 289-cu. in. V-8's of 200, 225 and 271 hp; 390-cu. in., 320-hp V-8. SelectShift Cruise-O-Matic Drive (automatic and manual combined) available with any engine. 4-Speed Manual Transmission available with any V-8.

*For price explanation, additional options, see pages 90-91.

Mustang Hardtop in Candyapple Red. Prices start as low as $2461.46.* Optional equipment on model shown includes: White Sidewall Tires, Wheel Covers, Rocker Panel Molding. Price of model equipped as shown: $2531.70.*

Mustang Convertible in Raven Black. Prices start as low as $2698.14.* Optional equipment on model shown includes: Wide-Oval Tires, Styled Steel Wheels, Exterior Decor Group, Side Accent Stripe, Rear Back Panel Grille, Rocker Panel Molding, 200-hp V-8, Interior Decor Group, Sports Steering Wheel, Convenience Control Panel, Console, Radio. Price of model equipped as shown: $3342.36.*

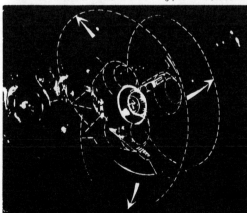

Optional Tilt-Away Steering Wheel automatically swings aside and up when you open driver's door. Wheel also can be tilted to nine different driving positions. $59.93*

Mustang Interiors have all-vinyl trim (available in seven color choices), deep-foam front bucket seats, color-keyed carpeting and full safety padding.

MUSTANG

FASTBACK 2+2

Optional Interior Decor Group
includes special trim, special lighting, and
many other luxury extras. Available
on all Mustangs $108.06.* ($94.36* on Conv.)

Here's a very special new Mustang with a unique fastback that slopes all the way aft. Those functional louvers on the sides of the top are controlled from inside by sliding levers and provide efficient Silent-Flo ventilation. The big rear window has tinted glass as standard equipment. The sporty interior seats two in bucket seats up front, and you still have room for two more passengers back aft.

In other respects, these 2 + 2's share the same features as other Mustangs. The list of standard equipment just won't stop (see preceding page). Included are all the standard Ford Motor Company Lifeguard-Design Safety Features . . . and you get Ford Motor Company's "3-Point Warranty Plan." Whatever transmission you choose—including the standard fully synchronized 3-speed job—has its shift lever floor-mounted. The standard engine is a zippy 120-hp Six and there are four optional V-8's to choose from—up to 320 hp. Transmission options include the sporty 4-speed stick shift and the new SelectShift Cruise-O-Matic which is both an automatic and a manual transmission. And other optional choices are available to put exactly your kind of personality into this car.

New options for 1967 include the convenient Tilt-Away Steering Wheel, Front Power Disc Brakes, AM/FM Radio, SelectAire Conditioner, Two Tone Paint, Wide-Oval Sports Tires, Shoulder Harnesses, Automatic Speed Control, and a Competition Handling Package. And there's a Sports Rear Deck option which converts the entire rear of the car to usable luggage space with an access door from the trunk. And that's only part of the story. Other options are shown on the following page . . . and there's a more complete listing on page 60.

Mustang Fastback 2+2 in Wimbledon White. Prices start as low as $2592.17.* Optional equipment on model shown includes: GT Equipment Group, Exterior Decor Group, Styled Steel Wheels, Lower Back Panel Grille, 320-hp V-8, Heavy-Duty 3-Speed Manual Transmission. Price of model equipped as shown: $3292.31.*

Convenience Control Panel
Includes reminder lights for parking brake, door ajar, low fuel and seat belts. $39.50.* Also illustrated:
Center Console $50.41* and **Stereo-Sonic Tape System** $128.49.* Available with AM radio only.

GT Equipment Group Makes Mustang even more the "Car-man's Car" with more performance gusto. Available on any model.
Includes Front Power Disc Brakes, 4" Fog Lamps,
Special Low-Restriction Dual Exhaust System and chromed "quad" exhaust outlets with the 271- or 320-hp V-8, GT Side Stripes,
GT ornamentation on gas cap, special Wide-Oval Tires,
higher-rate springs and shocks and stabilizer bar. $205.05*

MUSTANG Options

Mustang has the happy knack of becoming exactly your kind of car, depending on the equipment you choose.
Shown below are a few of the many choices. Others are listed on page 60. They all add convenience
and enjoyment to Mustanging—and they repay handsomely at trade-in time. Which makes them very good values indeed.

Power Front Disc Brakes
A brand-new Mustang option which combines the ease of power brakes with the high performance characteristics of front disc brakes. Rear brakes are husky, drum type. Available with V-8's only. $64.77*

AM/FM Radio Permits you to enjoy both AM and FM broadcasting. Has long-lived transistors, dependable printed circuit, and five push buttons which can be reset to new stations, when desired. (AM model $57.51*) $133.65*

Power Steering Takes 85% of the effort out of steering and still retains a precise "feel" of the road. Is especially helpful when parking in tight spots, and is a favored option among women drivers—and men too. $84.47*

Sport Deck Rear Seat This handy option for the 2+2 Fastback triples the luggage space. Rear seat folds flat so the entire rear of the car serves as trunk area. Access door from trunk permits carrying long items. $64.77*

Automatic Speed Control Holds cruising speeds anywhere between 25 and 80 mph. Has feature to resume speed after braking, if desired. Disengages with on-off switch or by touching brake pedal or turning off ignition. $71.30*

SelectShift Cruise-O-Matic Gives you the choice of automatic shifting or manual, whenever you want it. Leave the T-Bar in the Drive position, and it's fully automatic. Or shift it yourself through the three forward gears. Prices on page 60.

*For more complete list of optional equipment and price explanation, see pages 60 and 61.

How to make a Mustang GT

First, pick your V-8. Any of four big choices from the 289-cu. in. Challenger to a new 390-cu. in. Thunderbird Special. Then add the GT Equipment Group, and wonderful things happen.

Up front, a pair of 4-inch fog lamps are built into the grille. Tires are Wide-Oval Sports type, put more tread on the road for greater traction, look extra-low and sporty. Front power disc brakes take over to give you extra resistance against fade. The GT Equipment Group also includes the Special Handling Package: higher rate springs and shocks, huskier front stabilizer bar. (Competition Handling Package* may be substituted. Includes adjustable shocks, 3.25 rear axle, limited-slip differential, among others.) With both the big Cobra and Thunderbird Special V-8's, the Mustang GT exhaust system is a special low-restriction type, with dual mufflers and chromed "quad" outlets.

Final touches: accent stripes with "GT" (for stick shift) or "GTA" (for Cruise-O-Matic) and bright-metal rocker panel moldings.

*For complete details see your Ford Dealer

Ford's better ideas for sale—

Your Ford Dealer has ideas for sale right now that other cars won't have until next year—if then. Ideas like: SelectShift Cruise-O-Matic transmission, the automatic that works as a manual, too, even on 6-cylinder cars. Tilt-Away steering wheel swings aside, adjusts 9 ways. Convenience Control Panel warns if fuel is low or door's ajar. Lots more. Get these exclusives on hot-selling '67s like the Mustang Sports Sprint!

Mustang Sports Sprints, hardtop and convertible, come with special equipment at a special low price: ,
• Sporty hood vents with recessed turn indicators
• Whitewalls
• Full wheel covers
• Bright rocker panel moldings
• Chrome air cleaner
• Vinyl-covered shift lever—if you choose SelectShift
• Plus Mustang's long list of standard features
No wonder Mustang resale value is so high...
no wonder it outsells all its imitators combined!

1968 ideas at 1967 prices!

NOW! Special Savings on SelectAire Conditioner!

Here's an air-conditioning unit that isn't just "hung on." It's handsomely built into the instrument panel. So it saves space ... and looks as good as it keeps you feeling. You can get SelectAire right now at a special low price on a Mustang Sports Sprint or special Ford Galaxie models.

Also special savings on Galaxie 500 2- and 4-door hardtops.

SEE YOUR FORD DEALER TODAY!

MUSTANG · FALCON · FAIRLANE · FORD
THUNDERBIRD · CORTINA

33

IT'S SPRINT TIME!
MUSTANG SPORTS SPRINT SALE NOW GOING ON!

Specially equipped. Specially priced. Limited time only! See the latest, freshest versions of Mustang—with new GT hood, special wheel covers, in special Sprint Time colors. Now's the time to get special Sprint Time Sale values on all Mustangs—America's original (and still lowest priced) sports car with bucket seats. Sprint, don't walk, to your Ford dealer's today. IT'S SPRINT TIME. Time to take the Mustang Pledge!

the original
MUSTANG

take the
MUSTANG PLEDGE!

I WILL NOT...

I will not sell tickets to all the people who want to ride in my '67 Mustang.

I will not keep the neighbors up all night by playing my Mustang's stereo tape player.

I will not yawn when people talk about the performance of other cars.

I will not show off my Mustang's overhead console by turning on its map lights (at least, not in the daytime, anyway).

I WILL...

I will tell the truth about my Mustang's low price and not let people think I paid extra for bucket seats, vinyl interior, plush carpeting and all those other no-cost extras.

I will spend the money I save with Mustang on a good cause...myself.

I will love, honor and obey the Convenience Control Panel when its lights tell me to fasten seat belts and release the parking brake.

I will stick to my diet even though my Mustang's Tilt-Away steering wheel is so adjustable.

I will keep the "helpless-female" look by shifting manually only when I'm driving alone. All other times I will let the SelectShift work automatically.

I will catch up on my diary...one of these days.

MUSTANG *Ford*

MUSTANG, bred first to be first, still has all the great features that made it America's runaway success car.

How do you add excitement to the most exciting new car in a generation? This year we've given our three Mustang models— hardtop, convertible and fastback 2+2— racy new body . . . wider tread . . . a wider range of engines from the strong 200-cubic-inch Six to a new 390-cubic-inch V-8 that develops 320 horsepower.

We've added fresh options so Mustang is more than ever designed to be designed by you. Features like a Tilt-Away steering wheel that swings out of your way when you open the door, and tilts to nine different driving positions. Built-in heater/air conditioner, front disc power brakes, Super-Wide Oval tires for better-than-ever Mustang road-holding, and a new exterior decor group that will add greater distinctiveness to any Mustang model for '67.

What did we keep? We kept the standards that made Mustang famous in the first place: bucket seats, wall-to-wall carpeting, 3-speed stick shift (fully synchronized this year), courtesy lighting, and rich vinyl trim. Plus all of the Ford Motor Company Lifeguard-Design Safety Features. But most particularly, we kept that classic lean, adventurous Mustang look.

Come back to your Ford Dealer for a second look at the '67 Mustangs. Take a test drive, too, and see for yourself why we say Mustang is bred first to be first.

Mustang Hardtop, 2+2 with optional GT equipment group, and Convertible with exterior decor group option

Optional Mustang interior decor group includes seat inserts of comfort-weave vinyl, special instrument panel trim.

Optional Tilt-Away steering wheel moves over when you open driver's door, adjusts to 9 driving positions.

1967 Mustang Specifications

Color and Upholstery Selections: Pick your favorite color from 16 brilliant new Super Diamond Lustre Enamel single tones. Counting standard and optional choices, there are a total of 20 all-vinyl trims for the hardtop, 18 for 2+2, 16 for convertible. Your Ford Dealer will be happy to show you samples of new Mustang colors & upholsteries.

Engines (see chart for availability): **200-cu. in. Six—** 120 hp; 3.68 bore x 3.13" stroke, 0.0 to 1 comp. ratio; 7 main bearings; reg. fuel; single-barrel carb.; auto. choke; self-adj. valves with hydraulic lifters.

289-cu. in. Challenger V-8— 200 hp; 4.00" bore x 2.87" stroke; 9.3 to 1 comp. ratio; reg. fuel; 2-barrel carb.; auto. choke; self-adj. valves with hydraulic lifters.

289-cu. in. Challenger Special V-8— 225 hp; 4.00" bore x 2.87" stroke; 9.8 to 1 comp. ratio; 4-barrel carb.; prem. fuel. Other specifications same as Challenger V-8 above.

289-cu. in. Cobra V-8— 271 hp; 4.00" x 2.87" stroke 10.0 to 1 comp. ratio; prem. fuel; 4-barrel carb.; manual choke; solid valve lifters; dual exhaust.

390-cu. in. Thunderbird Special V-8— 320 hp; 4.05" bore x 3.78" stroke; 10.5 to 1 comp. ratio; prem. fuel; 4-barrel carb.; auto. choke; self-adj. valves; oil cap'y, incl. filter, 5 qt.; dual exhaust.

Engine Features: 6000-mile (or 6-month) full-flow disposable-type oil filter; replaceable dry element air cleaner; 190° thermostat; 12-volt electrical system with 38-amp. alternator; 42-amp. alternator on High Performance V-8; 54-plate, 45 amp-hr battery; weatherproof ignition; positive-engagement starter; fully aluminized muffler and tailpipe. All engines are electronically mass-balanced for long-lived smoothness.

13 Mustang Power Teams

Engines	Transmissions
200-Cu. In. Six*	S*, C
289-Cu. In. Challenger V-8	S*, C, 4
289-Cu. In. Challenger Special V-8	S*, C, 4
289-Cu. In. Cobra V-8	4*, C
390-Cu. In. Thunderbird Special V-8	S*, C, 4

Standard equipment; all others optional

Transmission Key:
S — Synchro-Smooth Drive (fully synchronized 3-speed manual)
C — Cruise-O-Matic Drive   4 — 4-Speed Manual

Manual Transmissions (see chart for availability): **Synchro-Smooth Drive.** Synchronized manual shifting in all three forward gears; clash-free downshifting to low while under way. Floor-mounted stick, standard "H" pattern.

4-Speed Manual. Sports-type close-ratio transmission, synchronized in all forward gears; floor-mounted stick.

SelectShift Cruise-O-Matic Drive: Lets you drive fully automatic or shift manually through the gears. Three forward speeds, one reverse. Effective engine braking in low gear (1) for better control on grades and hills. Quadrant sequence (P-R-N-D-2-1).

Rear Axle: Semi-floating hypoid rear axle; straddle-mounted drive pinion (V-8's). Permanently lubricated wheel bearings.

Front Suspension: Angle-Poised Ball-Joint type with coil springs mounted on upper arms. 36,000-mile (or 3-year) lube intervals. Strut-stabilized lower arms. Link-type, rubber-bushed ride stabilizer.

Rear Suspension: Longitudinal, 4-leaf springs with rubber-bushed front mounts, compression-type shackles at rear. Asymmetrical, variable-rate design with rear axle located forward of spring centers for anti-squat on takeoff. Diagonally mounted shock absorbers.

Steering: Recirculating ball-type steering gear provides easy handling. Permanently lubricated steering linkage joints. Overall steering ratio 25.4 to 1 (power steering 20.3 to 1). Turning diameter 38 ft.

Brakes: New dual hydraulic brake system with dual master cylinder, separate lines to front and rear brakes. Self-adjusting, self-energizing design. Composite drums grooved for extra cooling: 9″ (Six), 10″ (V-8's). Total lining areas: 131 sq. in. (Six), 154 sq. in. (V-8's).

Tires: Tubeless, blackwall with Tyrex rayon cord, 4-ply rating. Safety-type rims. Tire size—6.95 x 14.

Dimensions & Capacities: Length 183.6″; width 70.9″; height: hardtop 51.6″, fastback 51.8″, convertible 51.6″; wheelbase 108″; treads 58″; trunk luggage volume (cu. ft.): hardtop 9.2, convertible 7.7 (top down), fastback 5.1 (18.5 with optional rear seat folded down); fuel 17 gal.

Approximate Weights: Mustang Hardtop, 2732 lb. (Six), 2920 lb. (V-8); Mustang Fastback 2+2, 2759 lb. (Six), 2947 lb. (V-8); Mustang Convertible, 2892 lb. (Six), 3080 lb. (V-8).

Mustang "Worth More" Features mean more driving pleasure from your '67 Mustang today . . . more in resale value at trade-in. "Worth More" features include: aluminum scuff plates, seat side shields, parallel-action electric windshield wipers, curved side glass, suspended accelerator, brake and clutch pedals, deep-dish design steering wheel with chrome horn ring, dual sun visors with retention clips, front arm rests, coat hooks, 2-position door checks, counterbalanced hood and rear deck lid and many, many more.

24,000-Mile or 24-Month U.S. Warranty: Throughout Mustang is *total-car* quality which makes possible this warranty. Ford Motor Company warrants to owners as follows: That for 24,000 miles or for 24 months, whichever comes first, free replacement, including related labor, will be made by Ford Dealers of any part with a defect in workmanship or material. Tires are not covered by the warranty; appropriate adjustments will be made by tire companies. Owners will remain responsible for normal maintenance services, routine replacement of parts, such as filters, spark plugs, ignition points, wiper blades, brake or clutch linings, and normal deterioration of soft trim and appearance items. The warranty referred to herein is applicable to products normally operated in the U.S.A. and Canada.

Twice-a-Year Maintenance: '67 Mustangs are designed to go 6,000 miles (or 6 months) between oil changes and minor chassis lubrications; 36,000 miles (or 3 years,

whichever comes first) between major chassis lubes. Other Mustang service savings: 36,000-mile (or 2-year) engine coolant-antifreeze, self-adjusting brakes, long-life Sta-Ful battery, shielded alternator, rust- and corrosion-resistant aluminized muffler, galvanized vital underbody parts. Mustang needs so little service it's just good sense to see that it gets the best — at your Ford Dealer's. His factory-trained mechanics and special tools add up to the greatest service combination you'll ever find for your Mustang!

Prices: Mustang includes heater-defroster as standard equipment. However heater-defroster may be deleted on car order if desired at an appropriate price reduction. All optional equipment and accessories, illustrated or referred to as options, optional or available are at extra cost. For the price of the Mustang with the equipment you desire, see your Ford Dealer.

The illustrations and product information contained herein were current at the time this publication was approved for printing. However, in order to continue to offer the finest automotive products available, Ford Motor Company reserves the right to change specifications, designs, models or prices without notice and without liability for such changes.

You're ahead in a
FORD

MUSTANG · FALCON · FAIRLANE · FORD · THUNDERBIRD

Mustang Sprint. Special version of America's
original low-priced sporty car.

NOW ON SALE!

New low-priced Mustang Sprints.

Right now, your Ford Dealer has limited-edition Mustang Sprints on sale—special versions of the original, low-priced sporty car. We've put an even lower price on them. And your Ford Dealer is making special efforts to move them. Fast!

Look at the extras you get at special savings:

- GT stripes
- Special wheel covers
- Special exterior trim
- Flip-open gas cap
- Plus standard Mustang features like bucket seats, floor-mounted stick shift, and more

Order V-8 power and you can also save on:

- Wide-oval white sidewall tires
- Styled steel wheels
- GT fog lamps

Come in and see the low-priced Mustang Sprints—the other Mustangs, too. Your Ford Dealer has a very attractive price tag on *every one* of them. And they're going to go the way Mustangs always do. Beautifully and quick!

See the light. The switch is on to Ford!

Ford ...has a better idea.

GT/CS. California Special Mustang. Limited edition.
Inspiration by Shelby GT. But priced like a Mustang.
Look at all the special equipment that's standard:
Blackout grille. Rectangular fog lamps. Functional

louvered hood
signals. Shelby
sassy spoiler, full
horizontal taillights.
cap. On the sides,
scoops with "GT/CS"
stripes. Naturally, GT/CS
other standard that's made
Bucket seats. Leather-smooth
Carpeting. Floor shift. And many

DESIGNED TO BE DESIGNED INTO YOUR PERSONAL GT/CS

9-position Tilt-Away Wheel adjusts to you

For openers, Full-Width Seat and Decor Group

Two-Tone Hood goes with any Mustang color

Styled Steel Wheels. Wire-Style or Deluxe Whe

Best of all, you can "customize" a GT/CS into your own one-of-a-kind Mustang. It's done with Mustang's wide array of options. Make it posh. Sporty. Out of this world. Decorate it. Automate it. Some tempting options shown below. More where those came from. California made it happen! Make Mustang GT/CS happen to you *now* at your Ford Dealer's!

with integral turn
-style rear end — a
-edge striping. Wide
Pop-open gas
simulated air
insignia. Special
includes every
Mustang famous.
vinyl trim.
more.

Stereo Tape System

Vinyl Roof Covering

Four V-8's—up to 390 cubes!

Fingertip Speed Control

Quad Exhausts (GT Group)

SelectAire Conditioner

el Covers

Wide-ovals come with either Radial or Bias Ply

Power Front Discs

4-Speed Stick Shift

Built-in Tachometer

2-in-1 SelectShift

California made it happen
MUSTANG GT/CS

BRANDED MUSTANG ORDER FORM

Our dealership wishes to participate in the "Branded Mustang," Traffic-building Promotion. We understand that each Vinyl Top Kit includes: one pre-cut, hand-sewn Vinyl Top, two "C" Pillar Emblems, one set of Thoroughbred Stripes, two chrome "C" Pillar Side Moldings and Mastic material for top installation.

IMPORTANT: Pattern numbers refer to illustrations in Plans Book. Please be sure to list quantities in "A" or "B" columns.
"A" denotes kits for 1967-1968 Mustangs!
"B" denotes kits for 1965-1966 Mustangs!

Place number of kits desired in boxes adjacent to code numbers.

Pattern	1967/68	1965/66	Pattern	1967/68	1965/66	Pattern	1967/68	1965/66
L 648	A-01	B-02	SD 202	A-11	B-12	CN 876	A-21	B-22
L 950	A-03	B-04	DE 739	A-13	B-14	BL 450	A-23	B-24
L 794	A-05	B-06	DE 397	A-15	B-16	CN 253	A-25	B-26
BL 761	A-07	B-08	CT 918	A-17	B-18	CN 601	A-27	B-28
CT 318	A-09	B-10	CN 577	A-19	B-20	CN 745	A-29	B-30

Please specify quantity and color of Thoroughbred stripes. (Thoroughbred stripes may be shipped separately.)

☐ Red #31   ☐ White #32   ☐ Black #33   ☐ Blue #34   ☐ Gold #35

TOTAL number of kits ordered_____ @ $47.25 each; TOTAL $_____

☐ Ford Motor Company is hereby authorized to charge my Parts Account for this order plus prepaid transportation charges and applicable state and/or local taxes.

SHIP TO: Please print or type

Dealership Name_____ Parts Account No._____

Address_____

City_____ State_____ Zip_____

Dealer Signature_____ Title_____

FORWARD ONE COPY TO: DSI CORPORATION, P. O. BOX 1000, PLYMOUTH, MICHIGAN 48170

Keep one copy for your records.

45

1969-1970

The greatest choice of high performance models and engines in its history characterized Mustang's 1969 lineup.

Debuting on August 28, 1968, the new Mustang's wheelbase was unchanged at 108 inches but another 3.8 inches of front overhang was added to extend overall length to 187.4 inches. Key styling changes included a more sharply angled (by another 2.2%) windshield, ventless front windows and a revamped front end appearance featuring four headlamps and a black, injection-molded plastic grille. For the first time the Mustang's grille was devoid of the winsome corral and galloping mustang feature. Instead, a simple mesh insert was used along with a variation of the side body logo that had graced Mustangs in previous years. The rear taillights continued to feature a triple lenses arrangement on either side but their surfaces were now flat rather than curved. Due to thinner doors and a very modest 0.1 inch increase in body width the new Mustang offered increases in front hip and shoulder room of 1.6 and 2.6 inches respectively.

Replacing the 2+2 model was a new SportsRoof variation of the fastback body style. The 2+2's C-pillar mounted air extractors were not carried over for 1969. Instead, swing-out rear quarter windows were standard.

The initial performance-oriented Mustang model, the Mach I, retailed for $3,122, with a two-barrel, 220 hp, 351 cid V-8 as its standard engine. This engine was a raised block version of the 302 cid V-8 with a 1/2 inch increase in stroke. Also included in its base price was Ford's "competition-type" suspension, F70-14 wide oval white sidewall tires on slotted wheels with plain hub centers, a pop-open gas cap plus a special sound insulation package which included 55 pounds of additional sound deadening material.

The Mach I was available only in the SportsRoof body style and featured mid-body-height side stripes, as well as striping along the top of the rear spoiler and the quarter panel extensions. A flat-black finish was applied to the hood region, which was equipped with exposed hold-down pins and a non-functional air scoop. Rounding out the Mach I's exterior trim package were twin body-color racing style side mirrors, rocker panel molding, a pop-up gas cap and tinted rear window. The special status of the Mach I in the 1969 Mustang line was enhanced by its interior appointments, which were highlighted by standard high-back bucket seats available in a choice of three knitted vinyls. Simulated teak trim was applied to the instrument panel, console and door insert. Other standard Mach I features included bright floor pedals, tachometer, clock and trip odometer and lower door mounted safety/courtesy lights. A Mach I nameplate was also installed on the passenger's side dash panel.

Four engines were optional for the Mach I, beginning with the 351 cid Cleveland V-8 with a four-barrel carburetor, 9.5:1 compression ratio and 250 hp at 4600 rpm. Its cost was a modest $25.91. Both this engine and the base 351 V-8 had a three-speed manual gearbox as their standard transmission. The only 390 cid V-8 in the Mustang engine lineup with 320 hp was offered for $99.74. Two versions of Ford's 428 cid Cobra Jet (with or without ram air induction and priced respectively at $224.12 and $357.46) served as the ultimate in Mach I engine choices. Both were credited with 335 hp at 5200 rpm and a 10.6:1 compression ratio. Carburetion was by a four-barrel, 735 cfm Holley. Installation of either of these engines required the purchase of either the four-speed manual or C-6 Cruise-O-Matic. All Mach I Mustangs except those powered by the base engine were equipped with a dual exhaust system. The high speed potential of the Mach I was aptly demonstrated by a team of drivers led by Mickey Thompson at Bonneville in September, 1968. A total of three Mach I's established 295 new records including an average in excess of 157 mph for 24 hours.

Although it followed Chevrolet's Z/28 to the marketplace, the Boss 302 was soon acclaimed as one of the most exciting Mustangs ever offered by Ford. This SportsRoof bodied Mustang carried a price tag of $3,415 and was described by Ford as the "nearest thing to a Trans-Am Mustang that you can bolt a license plate onto." Conservatively rated at 290 hp, its 302 cid engine was equipped with Cleveland cylinder heads with extremely large 2.23 inch intake valves, and an aluminum high-rise manifold fitted with a 780 cfm Holley four-barrel carburetor. A wide-ratio, four-speed manual transmission was standard and during the model run a Hurst Competition Shifter replaced the Ford version initially used. The Boss 302's standard rear axle was a 3.50:1 Cobra Jet 428 "Daytona" version with 3.91:1 and 4.30:1 ratio also offered. Suspension modifications included stiffer springs, 0.94 inch front stabilizer bar and staggered rear shocks. Goodyear F60-15 polyglas tires, mounted in 7-inch wide Magnum 500 wheels were standard.

The use of this tire/wheel combination required special front and rear fenders with revised wheel openings for the Boss 302. The resulting appearance change was further enhanced by the removal of the artificial rear quarter air scoop, the installation of a 4-inch wide front spoiler and the application of matte black paint on the 302's hood, rear deck and outer headlight region. A distinctive side stripe whose shape reversed that of the 1968 GT option carried a "Boss 302" label on its leading edge.

Among the options available for the Boss 302 was a rear spoiler ($19.48), high back bucket seats ($84.25) and a limited slip differential ($63.51). In addition, distinctive "Sport Slats," hinged at the top to allow for rear window cleaning, were available for $128.28. Total output of Boss 302 Mustangs was 1,934.

Entering production in mid-January 1969 was the Boss 429. Ford admitted it "went a little ape" with this Mustang. With a gaping ram-air hood scoop, front spoiler and F60-15 Goodyear polyglas tires on 7-inch chrome rims, it was one of history's rarest Mustangs, as only 852 were built during the 1969 model run. Its engine was closely related to Ford's 429 V-8 used in Nascar competition. Its technical highlights included 4-bolt main bearings, forged steel crankshaft, aluminum heads, a 735 cfm Holley four-barrel and an aluminum high-riser manifold. Ford said that all the 429's features "add up to 375 horsepower and that's understating it considerably." Mandatory options for the Boss 429 included a heavy-duty four-speed manual transmission, a 3.91:1 locking rear axle and manual disc brakes. In this form the Boss 429 retailed for $4,798.

With the competition version of the Boss 302 winning the Trans Am championship and Mach I production totalling 72,458 (output of all Mustangs was 299,824), the Mustang not only still was America's first choice in pony cars in 1969 but a worthy competitor to any entry in the muscle car sweepstakes.

Debuting on September 3, 1969, the 1970 Mustangs had a model year production run of only 190,727 units, which was a drop of nearly 110,000 cars from the level of 1969. Styling changes were minor. The false rear quarter panel scoops were removed and a single headlamp system was adopted. The area where the outer pair of the superseded four lamp setup had been located was now occupied by two, stacked, non-functional air intakes. A broad grille with an insert of thin vertical and horizontal bars used the 1969 grille emblem as its centerpiece. Other distinctive features of the 1970 Mustang included higher mounted front side marker lights, recessed taillight lenses, high-backed bucket seats and a two-spoke steering wheel as standard equipment.

Once again the Mach I, Boss 302 and Boss 429 were the Mustang models oriented towards the performance enthusiast. The Model 63C Mach I (base priced at $327) continued to have the 2V (two-barrel caburetor) 351 cid V-8 as its standard power plant with either of the two 428 V-8s or a new 300 hp, 4V 351 Cleveland V-8 optional. The 428 Cobra Jet V-8 with ram air listed for $522, while the normal aspired version was priced at $457. The 351 option was offered at $194.

The 428 engines could be linked to a Drag Package with either a 3.91:1 Traction-Lok differential for $155 or a more costly, $207 Detroit Locker, 4.30:1 version. Both variations included an engine oil cooler, cap screw connecting rods plus modified crankshaft and flywheel.

Mach I Mustangs were easily identified by their black center hood stripe which was bracketed on either side by thinner stripes whose length was broken by engine size numerals on each side of the standard non-functional hood scoops. Mach I Mustangs with black or dark green bodies had white rather than black striping. Also giving the Mach I a distinctive appearance were its grille-mounted rectangular sport lights and dark argent extruded aluminum rocker panel molding with a prominent Mach I I.D. At the rear, die cast Mach I lettering separated two large stripes positioned along the rear edge of the built-in spoiler. A black, honey-combed back panel applique separated the Mach I's taillights. Principal interior features of the Mach I included simulated wood grain appliques on the dash panel and console, and a three-spoke rim blow wheel. Total output of Mach I Mustangs was 40,970.

The Boss 302, whose production was a respectable 6,318 units, continued to be powered by the potent 290 hp, 302 cid V-8. Standard equipment included a new rear stabilizer bar, a choice of either a wide or close ratio four-speed manual transmission with a Hurst shifter, staggered rear shocks and 15 inch wheels on which were mounted F60-15 fiberglass belted tires. Magnum 500 wheels were optional at $129.

Giving the Boss 302 instant identity on the American road was a revised exterior striping arrangement. The matte black hood section was narrower and, like that on the Mach I, was joined by thinner stripes on either side. Those on the Boss 302 made an abrupt 90 degree turn at the base of the windshield to run down the front fender and then, after another sharp turn, extended the remaining length of the body. Prominent Boss 302 lettering and numerals were placed high on the front fender line. At the rear, both the lower back panel and taillight bezels, as well as the deck lid, were finished in black. The imposing appearance that resulted was further enhanced by the optional $65 black finished sport slats.

Considerably more costly than the $3,720 Boss 302 (which was technically an option package for the $2,771 SportsRoof Mustang) was the Boss 429, which with all mandated options was priced at $4,932. The Boss 429 was discontinued during the model year and only 498 were produced. Unlike 1969, when some of the early 429s were fitted with hydraulic lifters, all 1970 Boss 429 engines had mechanical lifters. As in 1969, the exterior appearance of the Boss 429 was, in relationship to its potency, restrained. The black finished hood scoop was still operated by the driver and such items as an engine oil cooler, trunk mounted battery and Magnum 500 wheels with F60-15 tires were continued.

Mustang catalogues continued the vertical format of 1968 into 1969 and 1970. Mustangs continued to play a prominent role in the full-line Ford literature, as well, although declining musclecar sales began to put a crimp in that. Exceprts from the 1969 "Ford Buyer's Digest" catalogue appear (see pages 48-49), along with those from the "Performance Buyer's Digest" catalogue (see pages 52-53) and a "Performance Appeal" accessories folder. A Boss 302 magazine ad is reproduced on pages 54-55. An ad extolling Mustang performance successes appears on page 56. For 1970, the "Ford Buyer's Digest" Mustang spread is reproduced on pages 58-59, while the Mustang section from the 1970 "Peformance Buyer's Digest" appears on pages 60-63. Mustang 1970 catalogue specifications appear on page 57.

'69 MUSTANG

Five all-new...
livelier, sportier than ever!

Mustang, the original. Zooms in with 5 all-new models, headed by the power-primed Mach I. Zesty 351-cu. in. V-8, racy hood dome, outside pin-type hood lock latches, belted tires, steel wheels, racing mirrors, high-back buckets, and more—all standard. A luxurious new Grandé, lavishly appointed, including teak-toned highlights on dash and door panels, buckets trimmed in vinyl and hopsack, wire-style wheel covers, and more. Mustang Convertible—top-down magic. An exciting new Mustang SportsRoof—rear spoiler, racy styling, with-it action. Mustang Hardtop, newest version of the one that started it all. Each model lower, longer, wider, roomier. And you get buckets, floor shift, plush carpeting—standard. Choice of 7 optional engines, including the 428 4V Cobra Jet Ram-Air V-8.

Facts about the 1969 Mustang. STANDARD FEATURES include: 351-cu. in., 2V 250-hp V-8 on Mach I; 200-cu. in., 115-hp Six on other models; 3-Speed Manual Transmission with Floor-Mounted Shift; Bucket Seats; Carpeting; Courtesy Lighting. Reversible Keys, "Keyless" Locking. **OPTIONS INCLUDE:** SelectShift; Tilt-Away Steering Wheel; SelectAire Conditioner; AM/FM Stereo Radio, Styled Steel Wheels, Power Front Disc Brakes, Fingertip Speed Control, Intermittent Windshild Wipers, GT Equipment, many more.

Basic specifications: Length—187.4"; Width—71.3"; Height—Hardtops 51.3"; Convertible 51.2"; SportsRoof and Mach I 50.4"; Wheelbase—108.0"; Tread—58.5"; Trunk Luggage Volume—Hardtops 9.8 cu. ft.; Convertible 8.0 cu. ft.; SportsRoof and Mach I 5.3 cu. ft.; Fuel—20 gal.

A. Mustang Hardtop, the original, the one that started it all. Sportier than ever. Quick, precise handling, surprisingly economical.

B. Mustang Mach I. Wild newcomer with hood dome, spoiler, styled steel wheels, belted wide treads. Shown in Candyapple Red. **Mustang SportsRoof,** new 2+2 version, more vibrant and vivacious than before, is also available.

C. Mustang Mach I Interior—High-backed buckets, wood-rimmed 3-spoke wheel, console, teak-toned highlights, electric clock, floor-mounted 4-speed stick.

D. Mustang Grandé—The luxury Mustang. Neat stripes, wire-style wheel covers, racing-style mirrors, bright highlights. Shown here in Winter Blue.

E. Mustang Grandé Interior—Luxury hopsack cloth and vinyl seat trim. Teak-toned highlights on instrument panel and doors. Special sound insulation.

F. Mustang Convertible, with on-the-move magic. Five-ply vinyl top, clear vinyl backlite. When it comes to magic, Mustang makes it happen.

THE COMPLETE DRESS-UP PACKAGE

Take a Mustang or Fairlane of any year . . . add the complete DRESS UP KIT: the easy "bolt-on" CYCOLAC HOOD SCOOP . . . the HOOD PIN KIT with its special adhesive backing eliminating sheet metal screws . . . and your choice of black, blue or white RACING STRIPES. If you're half way there, pick up what you need as separate items.

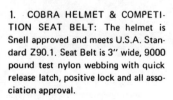

1.   COBRA HELMET & COMPETI-TION SEAT BELT: The helmet is Snell approved and meets U.S.A. Standard Z90.1. Seat Belt is 3" wide, 9000 pound test nylon webbing with quick release latch, positive lock and all association approval.

2.   COBRA BUTANE LIGHTER: A fine accessory that needs no special adapter for filling . . . lightweight . . .

matte black with Cobra plaque.

2. COBRA or MUSTANG FOBS: The smart companionables. Imported leather with the colorful cloisonne emblem makes this a fine keeper of the keys.

3.   NEW COBRA DRIVING JACKET: Advertised in Playboy. New - yet-to-be copied 100% double gauge Oxford nylon. Big ring zip-cuffs and front. Comes with Cobra Patch. Available with zip in liner.

4. COBRA JUMP SUIT

A specially designed outfit made of 65% key. Wash it and wash it and wash it! and comfort. Distinctive striped sleeves, as shown above. The item for singles, front or back-belted, it's doubly comfor-

Lastly, to light the way install your own pair of LUCAS LIGHTS in either Long Range or Special Fog. Check your state for approval. For the finishing touch add the special "COBRA 15" x 7" (MAG) WHEEL." See the performance man at your Ford Dealer.

Fortrel Polyester. Hi-Performance is the Front and back-belted for added versatility Cobra patch and Cobra name on the back ubles or teams. Since it can be worn either able and driver-mechanic designed.

5. COBRA WINDBREAKER: This is THE item. 100% nylon - not to be confused with the typical cotton types. The ideal club jacket.

6. KNOBS & T-BARS: A new look for a proven item. Shift knobs and T-bars in walnut with either Cobra or Mustang insert designs. Or grip the

vinyl Leather Grained knob with the continental feel.

7. WHEEL GLOVE: Couple your interior appointments with this genuine leather wheel glove. It's the GT feel that "performance" is all about.

1969 Mustang Mach 1 with 428 CID 4V Cobra Jet Ram-Air V-8

Ford's Exclusive "Shaker" scoop actually protrudes through the hood — rams air directly into the carburetor under full throttle

Mach 1 Specifications—*Standard engine:* 351 CID 2V V-8. Bore and stroke, 4.00 x 3.50 in. 9.5:1 compression, regular fuel. 250 hp at 4600 rpm. Torque 355 lbs-ft at 2600 rpm *Optional engines:* 351 CID 4V V-8, compression 10.7:1, premium fuel, 290 hp at 4800 rpm. Torque 385 lb. at 3200 rpm. 390 CID 4V V-8, compression 10.5:1, premium fuel, 320 hp at 4600 rpm. Torque 427 lb. at 3200 rpm. 428 CID 4V V-8. All 4V engines have dual exhausts. *Transmissions:* Std. 3-speed fully synchronized floor shift, ratios 2.42:1, 1.61:1, 1.00:1. Optional 4-speed floor shift, ratios 2.78:1, 1.93:1, 1.36:1, 1.00:1. SelectShift, ratios 2.46:1, 1.46:1, 1.00:1. *Brakes:* 10.0 in. drums, lining area 173.3 sq. in. *Wheels:* Chrome styled steel, 14 x 6 with wide-oval belted white side-wall tires. Optional FR70 radial ply. *Suspension:* GT handling with 351 & 390 CID V-8's, competition HD with 428 CID V-8. **Mustang GT Specifications**—*Standard engine:* 351 2V V-8 (see Mach 1 specifications). *Optional engines:* 351 4V V-8, 290 hp, 390 CID 4V V-8, 320 hp. 428 CID 4V V-8, 335 hp (see page P2). 428 CID Cobra Jet Ram-Air 4V V-8, 335 hp with through-the-hood functional air scoop (see page P2). All 4V engines have dual exhausts. *Transmissions:*

Standard 3-speed fully synchronized floor shift. Ratios 2.42:1, 1.61:1, 1.00:1. Optional 4-speed floor shift, ratios 2.78:1, 1.93:1, 1.36:1, 1.00:1. SelectShift, ratio 2.46:1, 1.46:1, 1.00:1. *Brakes:* 10.0 in. drums, lining area 173.3 sq. in. *Wheelbase:* 108.0". Overall length 187.4". *Weights:* Hardtop—3243 lb., SportsRoof—3267 lb., Convertible—3353 lb. *Wheels:* Styled steel, 14 x 6 with wide-oval belted white sidewall tires. Optional FR70 radial ply tires. *Suspension:* GT handling with 351 & 390 CID V-8's; competition HD with 428 CID V-8; **Mach 1 and Mustang GT Options:** 351 CID 4V V-8 (290 hp); 390 CID 4V V-8 (320 hp); 428 CID 4V V-8 (335 hp) (390 and 428 CID require Cruise-O-Matic or 4-speed manual transmission; 428 CID 4V Cobra Jet Ram-Air V-8 (335 hp) (requires Cruise-O-Matic or close ratio 4-speed manual transmission and F70x14 wide-oval belted tires) • SelectShift Cruise-O-Matic Transmission—351 2V or 4V V-8 • 390 4V, 428 4V or 428 Cobra Jet V-8 • Four-Speed Manual—351 2V or 4V V-8—390, 428 and 428 CID Cobra Jet V-8 engines (includes tach & trip odometer) • Power Steering • Traction-Lok Differential • Power Front Disc Brakes • F70x14 Wide-Oval Belted Black Sidewall Tires with raised white letters to look like a performer.

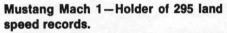

Mustang Mach 1—Holder of 295 land speed records.

This is the one that Mickey Thompson started with. From its wide-oval, belted tires to its wind tunnel designed SportsRoof, the word is "go." There's just one body — the same wind-splitting sheetmetal as the specially modified Mach 1 that screamed around Bonneville, clocking over 155, hour after hour, to break some 295 USAC speed and endurance records. Underneath that sleek, new shape is more Mustang than ever before. Standard are a new lightweight, free-breathing 2V 351 CID V-8, rated at 250 hp; handling suspension, simulated hood scoop, exposed lock pins and matte black hood, chrome styled steel wheels, and wide-oval belted white sidewall tires. In the high back bucket seat you sit behind a Rim-Blow deluxe steering wheel with integral horn rim switch, and look in dual color-keyed racing mirrors. Check the complete instrument cluster mounted in the simulated teakwood-grained panel. Shift the fully synchronized manual transmission from the center console. Then and only then, you'll begin to realize what kind of great machine you have.

Mustang GT—Stack extra performance on the Mustang you fancy.

Mustang's all-new GT's come in three sporty shapes—hardtop, convertible and SportsRoof. And all of them have a big slice of the all-out performance that has made our specially prepared Mustangs the big Trans Am gun over many a rough road course. The GT Equipment Group includes styled steel wheels, wide-oval belted white sidewall tires, simulated hood scoop and locking pins, special handling package, racing stripes, and more. Performance comes on strong with the new, lightweight 351 CID 2V 250-hp V-8.

1969 Mustang GT Hardtop

Nearest thing to a Trans-Am Mustang that you can bolt a license plate onto.

Boss 302

Our objective was to build a reasonably quick machine with a tight power to weight ratio. Power starts with a lightweight, precision-cast short-stroke 302 C.I.D. block. Top it with 10.5:1 heads with inclined 2.23″ intake and 1.71″ exhaust valves under aluminum rocker covers. Bolt on an aluminum high-riser manifold and a 780 CFM 4-barrel Holley carb. Add low-restriction headers and large-diameter dual exhausts. Fire it with dual-point ignition. You get 290 hp at 6000 easy revs. And it can be tuned for more.

Power gets to the road via a high-capacity 10.4″ clutch and a trigger-quick 4-speed box. There's a "Daytona" axle with a standard 3.50 ratio. You can order it with a 3.50, 3.91 or 4.30 locker axle if you're that kind of guy. Wheels are styled-steel 7″ rims with F60 x 15 fiber-glass belted tires. (These smokers are 2 inches wider than F70's. We had to flair the wheel wells a bit to get them on.) Quick-ratio steering, floating-caliper front disc power brakes, competition-

1969 Trans-Am Boss 302 Mustang

handling springs, shocks, front stabilizer bar and front spoiler are standard. Comes with a collapsible spare tire in case you're wondering about trunk space. One body only—'69 Mustang SportsRoof.

Options include rear spoiler, backlight louvers, power steering and chrome plated (15 x 7) styled steel wheels.

Objective accomplished. You're invited to inspect one at your Ford Dealer's Performance Corner. Also on display at various Trans-Am events coming up soon.

For your free copy of Ford's 1969 Performance Buyer's Digest, write:
Performance Digest, Department MT, P. O. Box 1000, Dearborn, Michigan 48121.

MUSTANG *Ford*

1969 Mustangs shatter 295 speed and endurance records.

All-new Mustang runs
24 hours nonstop at 157.663 m.p.h.

No American production car has ever gone so far so fast. In a single 24-hour run—the engine never stopped turning—the specially prepared and modified canary yellow 1969 Mustang SportsRoof screamed its way around the rutted 10-mile course at an average of 157.663 miles per hour. Driven by professional record-breaker Mickey Thompson and co-driver Danny Ongais, the sleek new Mustang, powered by a 302-cubic inch Ford V-8, went a distance of 3,783 miles in the 24 hours. Thompson's average speed was 17 miles per hour *faster* and the distance driven was 405 miles *farther* than the previous record. In the 24-hour period the yellow 1969 Mustang set over 100 American stock car records in the Class "C" Division for engines between 183 and 304 cubic inches as prescribed by the United States Auto Club. In another specially prepared 1969 Mustang SportsRoof, Thompson went on to break all standing and flying start records from 25 to 500 miles in Class B (305 to 488 cubic inch displacement). All these records make an undeniable statement about the new 1969 Mustang . . . never before has any car combined the performance to go so fast and the durability to do it for so long. What this means to you: The 1969 Mustangs are winners—at the track or on the turnpikes. See them in your Ford Dealer's Performance Corner.

NEW MUSTANG RECORDS
— (Partial listing) —

Class B (305 to 488 cu. in. displacement)
Flying Start—25, 50, 75, 100, 200, 250, 300, 400 and 500 kilometers
Flying Start—25, 50, 75, 100, 200, 250, 300, 400 and 500 miles

Standing Start—25, 50, 75, 100, 200, 250, 300, 400 and 500 kilometers
Standing Start—25, 50, 75, 100, 200, 250, 300, 400 and 500 miles

Class C (183 to 305 cu. in. displacement)
Flying Start—25, 50, 75, 100, 200, 250, 300, 400, 500, 1000, 2000, 3000, 4000, 5000 kilometers

Flying Start—25, 50, 75, 100, 200, 250, 300, 400, 500, 1000, 2000, 3000, 4000 miles

Standing Start—25, 50, 75, 100, 200, 250, 300, 400, 500, 1000, 2000, 3000, 4000, 5000 kilometers

Standing Start—25, 50, 75, 100, 200, 250, 300, 400, 500, 1000, 2000, 3000, 4000 miles

Flying Start—1-hour, 3-hour, 6-hour and 24-hour endurance
Standing Start—1-hour, 3-hour, 6-hour and 24-hour endurance

FORD
IT'S THE GOING THING!

All data certified by U.S. Auto Club

MUSTANG

The place you've got to go to see what's going on—your Ford Dealer!

facts on number one!

Color and Trim: 16 brilliant Super Diamond Lustre Enamel exterior finishes, and 6 standard vinyl interior trims, 6 optional knitted vinyl trims (Decor Group), 5 cloth and vinyl trims in Grandé. Also 2 Blazer cloth and vinyl colors.

ENGINES:

200 CID 1V Six—120 hp; 3.68" bore x 3.13" stroke; 8.8 to 1 comp. ratio; 7 main bearings; reg. fuel.

250 CID 1V Six—155 hp; 3.68" bore x 3.91" stroke; 9.0 to 1 comp. ratio; 7 main bearings; reg. fuel.

302 CID 2V V-8—220 hp; 4.00" bore x 3.00" stroke; 9.5 to 1 comp. ratio; regular fuel.

302 CID 4V "Boss"—290 hp; 4.00" bore x 3.00" stroke; 10.6 to 1 comp. ratio; premium fuel.

351 CID 2V V-8—250 hp; 4.00" bore x 3.50" stroke; 9.5 to 1 comp. ratio; regular fuel.

351 CID 4V V-8—300 hp; 4.00" bore x 3.50" stroke; 11.0 to 1 comp. ratio; premium fuel.

428 CID 4V Cobra V-8*—335 hp; 4.13" bore x 3.98" stroke; 10.6 to 1 comp. ratio; premium fuel.

428 CID Cobra Jet Ram-Air 4V V-8*—335 hp; 4.13" bore x 3.98" stroke; 10.6 to 1 compression ratio; premium fuel.

429 CID 4V "Boss" V-8—375 hp; 4.36" bore x 3.60" stroke; 10.5 to 1 comp. ratio; premium fuel.

*Optional Drag Pack includes Traction-Lok differential with 3.91 axle ratio or "No-Spin" locker with 4.30 axle ratio, plus these 428-cu. in. 4V engine modifications: engine oil cooler, cap screw connecting rods, modified crankshaft, flywheel and damper. Available with 428-cu. in. 4V non Ram-Air or Ram-Air V-8's.

Engine Features: 6000-mile (or 6-month) maintenance schedule with full-flow disposable type oil filter; dry element air cleaner; auto. choke; self-adjusting valves with hydraulic lifters (mechanical valves, Boss 429); 12-volt electrical system; 42-amp. alternator, 45 amp-hr battery with 250 thru 351 CID engines, 55-amp. with automatic transmission on 200, 351 engines; 55-amp. alternator and 80 amp-hr battery with 428's, 429.

TRANSMISSIONS:

3-Speed Manual: fully synchronized.

4-Speed Manual: sports-type w/Hurst Shifter®tm.

SelectShift Cruise-O-Matic Drive: 3-speed fully automatic transmission which may be used manually to hold first or second gear for engine braking, better hill control hauling trailers.

MUSTANG POWER TEAMS

Engines	Transmissions			
	3-Speed Manual	Select-Shift	4-Speed Manual Wide-Ratio	4-Speed Manual Close-Ratio
200 Six (120 hp)	X	X		
250 Six (155 hp)	X	X		
302 V-8 (220 hp)	X	X	X	
302 Boss (290 hp)			X	X
351 V-8 2V (250 hp)	X	X	X	X
351 V-8 4V (300 hp)	X	X	X	X
428 V-8 Cobra (335 hp)		X		X
428 V-8 Cobra Jet (335 hp)	X	X		X
429 Boss V-8 (375 hp)				X

Rear Axle: semi-floating hypoid type; permanently lubricated rear wheel bearings.

Front Suspension: angle-poised ball-joint type with coil springs; strut-stabilized lower arms; link-type stabilizer.

Rear Suspension: asymmetrical variable-rate design longitudinal 4-leaf springs. Diagonally mounted shocks.

Steering: recirculating ball-type, permanently lubricated. 25.45 to 1 overall ratio (20.48 to 1 power). Turning diameter 37.6 ft.

Brakes: dual hydraulic system with dual master cylinder. Self-adjusting, self-energizing design. Lining areas: 130.4 sq. in. (200 Six); 154.0 sq. in. (250 Six, 302 V-8); 173.3 sq. in. (351, 428's, 429); Boss 302, 232.0 sq. in. swept area.

Dimensions and Capacities: Length 187.4"; Width 71.7"; Height 51.5" (SportsRoof—50.6"); Wheelbase 108"; Track 58.5"; Trunk 8.3 cu. ft. (hardtop), 7.2 cu. ft. (SportsRoof), 7.2 cu. ft. (convertible). Fuel—20 gallons (in California, 22 gal. std.).

Weight: Hardtop—3080 lb.; SportsRoof—3104 lb.; Convertible—3190 lb.

STANDARD EQUIPMENT

Hardtop—Power Team: 200-cu. in. Big Six and fully synchronized 3-speed manual transmission • floor-mounted shift lever • color-keyed loop-pile carpeting • courtesy lights • cigarette lighter • reversible keys • keyless locking • heater/defroster • all-vinyl interior • curved side glass • high-back bucket seats • locking steering column • Hurst Shifter (with 4-speed man. trans.) • Twice-a-Year Maintenance • glove box • color-keyed headlining • printed circuit instrument panel • aluminized and stainless steel muffler • black or white paint stripe with engine numerals (351-, 428-, 429-cu. in. V-8's) • E78-14 fiberglass belted bias-ply BSW tires. Plus all FORD LIFEGUARD DESIGN SAFETY FEATURES.

Mustang Grandé—In addition to the features listed for Hardtop: special sound insulating package • special soft-ride suspension • luxury cloth and vinyl seat trim • molded door trim panels and courtesy lights • deluxe 2-spoke steering wheel • woodtone instrument panel appliques • electric clock • bright floor pedal trim • dual color-keyed racing mirrors including remote control LH mirror • dual bodyside paint stripe • black or white "Landau" vinyl roof covering • houndstooth check interior trim fabrics in 5 colors.

Convertible—In addition to Hardtop features listed for Hardtop: 5-ply manually operated vinyl top • clear vinyl backlite • color-keyed boot • easy-action top fastening latches • full-width rear seat • courtesy lights under instrument panel • glove compartment lock, wheel covers • rocker panel molding with vinyl insert • lower back panel applique • wheel lip molding.

SportsRoof: In addition to Hardtop features: integral rear deck spoiler • swing-out rear quarter windows • tinted glass backlite • courtesy lights under instrument panel, rear compartment.

Mustang Mach 1: In addition to Hardtop features listed previously: Power Team: 351-cu. in. 2V V-8 and fully synchronized 3-speed manual transmission • non-functional hood scoop/integral turn signal indicators • functional "shaker" hood scoop • competition suspension • outside color-keyed dual racing mirrors • knitted vinyl high-back bucket seats/accent stripes • console with wood-tone applique • Rim-Blow deluxe three-spoke steering wheel • Bright dual exhaust extensions • Hood lock pins • Honeycomb back panel applique • Wide-oval belted WSW tires • Pop-open gas cap • Dark argent extruded aluminum rocker panel molding • Deck lid tape stripe (Diecast "Mach 1") • Black or white painted hood and tape engine numerals • Die cast center deep dish sports wheel covers • simulated driving lamps • Woodgrain cluster with right-hand instrument panel applique • electric clock • Bright pedal pads • Molded door trim panels w/courtesy lights • NVH sound package • Carpet runners.

Mustang Boss 302: In addition to Hardtop and SportsRoof features listed above: Power Team: 302-cu. in. 4V V-8 engine rated at 290 hp and 4-speed manual transmission equipped with Hurst Shifter®tm • black taillamp bezels • black chrome backlite molding and headlamp castings • color-keyed dual racing mirrors • black hood and rear deck lid and black lower back panel • F-60-15 belted BSW tires w/ white letters • hub cap/trim ring • space saver spare • "C" stripes • Boss 302 tape identification on front fender (black only) • dual exhausts • quick ratio steering (16:1) • competition suspension including staggered rear shocks • special cooling package • 3.50 non-locking axle • front spoiler • 45 ampere battery • power front disc brakes.

Every 1970 Mustang includes these Ford Motor Company Lifeguard Design Safety Features: Dual hydraulic brake system with warning light • Glare reduced instrument panel padding, windshield wiper arms, steering wheel hub, rearview mirror/mirror mounting and windshield pillars • Energy-absorbing steering column, steering wheel, armrests and safety-designed door handles • Uni-Lock Safety Harness • Front and rear lap belts • Shoulder belts for front outboard occupants (except convertibles) • Turn indicators with lane-changing signal feature • Inside yield away rearview mirror • Energy-absorbing instrument panel with padding • Padded sun visors • Two-speed windshield wipers • Windshield washers • High strength laminate safety glass windshield • Double-yoke safety door latches and safety hinges • Emergency flasher • Backup lights • Side marker lights • Energy-absorbing front seat back tops with padding • Self-locking front seat backs • Safety-designed coat hooks (except convertibles) • Safety-designed radio control knobs and push buttons • Outside rearview mirror, driver's side • Safety rim wheel and load-rated tires • Corrosion-resistant brake lines • Uniform transmission shift quadrant • Parking lamps coupled with headlamps • Non-reversing odometer • Safety design front end structure • High-back seats • Safety glove box latch.

NOTE: Your new 1970 Mustang comes equipped with factory engineered and approved parts such as the dependable Autolite Sta-Ful battery, Autolite Power-Tip spark plugs, Autolite shock absorbers, and an Autolite 6000-mile oil filter. Be sure to specify genuine Autolite parts whenever replacement is necessary.

While the information shown herein was correct when approved for printing, Ford Division reserves the right to discontinue, or change at any time, specifications or designs without incurring any obligations. Some features shown or described are optional at extra cost.

MUSTANG HARDTOP

MUSTANG SPORTSROOF

MUSTANG CONVERTIBLE

MUSTANG GRANDE

MUSTANG MACH 1

MUSTANG BOSS 302

MUSTANG *Ford*

MUSTANG MACH 1 WITH OPTIONAL "SHAKER" HOOD SCOOP

MUSTANG
Number One

MACH 1 . . . when you like it hot. Whichever way you like it, Mustang's the Number One choice for '70. Best-selling sporty car ever, it now has new allure outside, new glamour inside, new power play under the hood. Like it hot? Try Mach 1 . . . a machine that likes to get out and go places. Life will never be the same, of course. Mach 1 magic does that. And no wonder. It's got standards like: a unique new grille and grille lamps; dual hood locks; black painted hood; hood scoop; E70-14 belted bias-ply white sidewall tires; new cast wheel covers; dual color-keyed racing mirrors; high-back bucket seats with knitted vinyl trim that stays cool and comfortable; under the hood a 351 2V V-8. Optional choices include: V-8's all the way up to the 428 Cobra Jet; "shaker" hood scoop; a close-ratio 4-speed transmission with Hurst Shifter®; adjustable rear spoiler; Sport Slats backlite louvers . . . and lots more.

GRANDE . . . when you like it rich. How about Grandé, the formal luxury model? Grandé elegance says formality can be fun and backs it up with a unique, distinctively crowned, black or white vinyl Landau roof, high-back foam-filled bucket seats, deluxe 2-spoke steering wheel, woodtone instrument panel and new houndstooth-check upholstery. Plus a wide array of luxury options like: SelectAire Conditioner; Full AM/FM Stereo Radio; Stereo Tape Deck; new Houndstooth Vinyl Roof in Blue or Green (to match interiors); and Tilt Steering Wheel.

MUSTANG GRANDE

MUSTANG GRANDE INTERIOR

MUSTANG BOSS 302

BOSS 302 . . . when you like it quick. This one goes like the wild wind. All-out performance for adventurous souls who want to rule the road. A high-output Boss 302 4V V-8 winds up 290 ferocious horses. It has belted wide-oval tires, hub cap/trim ring, a front spoiler, and a space saver spare tire. Available are hot extras like the "shaker" hood scoop, adjustable rear deck spoiler and Sport Slats (shown above), and the close-ratio 4-speed with Hurst Shifter®. Like all Mustangs, Boss is available in wild colors, too. And there's plenty more.

SPORTSROOF, HARDTOP, CONVERTIBLE . . . however you like it. Mustang is Number One to run with. And Mustang gives you so many ways to live it up economically. You get great standard features like: full carpeting; high-back bucket seats; sports-styled interiors; sweet, sassy 200 CID Six; 3-speed manual transmission; belted tires; anti-theft locking steering column; Twice-a-Year Maintenance, and a full quota of Ford's better ideas. There's a kaleidoscope of Mustang color choices, too. How does Grabber Green grab you? Grabber Orange? Grabber Blue? Bright Yellow? Vermilion? And there are 11 other Super Diamond Lustre Enamel color selections.

There's a host of Mustang options, too, so you can design your own exclusive Mustang — the car to suit *your* individual needs and personality. Start with the special Decor Group (includes Blazer Stripe seat trim, woodtoned instrument panel, dual racing mirrors and other sporty dress-up items), center Console, Power Front Disc Brakes, a big 250 CID Six or choice of seven V-8's, SelectShift, SelectAire Conditioner, to name a few. Live gloriously. Splurge modestly. Go with Number One.

Boss 302 – Son of Trans – Am.

The Mustang Boss 302 is what comes from winning those Trans-Am championships. From its 5-litre, F.I.A. sanctioned V-8 to its 16-to-1 steering, the Boss is designed to go quick and hang tight. The standard specs sound like a $9,000 European sports job instead of a reasonably priced, reliable American pony car. Boss 302 comes in just one body style— the wind-splitting SportsRoof shape. The engine is Ford's high output 302 CID 4V V-8, with new cylinder heads to permit canting the valves for better gas flow and larger diameter—2.18 intake, 1.71 exhaust. That's what gives you a big 290 horsepower from a small, lightweight 302 CID engine.

Choose either close or wide ratios on Boss 302's butter-smooth, fully synchronized 4-speed. We've made it an even quicker box by adding a T-handle Hurst Shifter.®

Brakes are power boosted, ventilated floating caliper front discs. When we tell you the suspension is competition type with staggered rear shocks to combat rear wheel hop on

Car and Driver Magazine says, "The Boss 302... may just be the new standard by which everything from Detroit must be judged."

Two Trans-Am Championships for Mustang taught us how to set up Boss 302.

Engine: 302 CID 4V V-8. (See back page for detailed engine specifications.) **Transmission:** 4-speed fully synchronized with Hurst Shifter®; standard wide ratios: 2.78:1, 1.93:1, 1.36:1, 1.0:1; optional close ratios: 2.32:1, 1.69:1, 1.29:1, 1.0:1.

Rear Axle: Heavy-duty, 9″ ring gear, standard ratio 3.50:1.

Brakes: Power-boosted floating caliper ventilated front disc brakes, diameter 11.3″; rear brakes 10″ drums. Swept area 282.5 sq. in.

Wheelbase: 108″. Overall length 187.4″, tread, front and rear 59.5″.

Suspension: Extra heavy-duty front coil and rear leaf springs, extra heavy-duty shock absorbers and front stabilizer bar, staggered rear shock absorbers, rear stabilizer bar.

Steering: Ratios, **Standard**—16:1 manual; **Optional**—16:1 power.

Wheels: 7″ rims. F60 x 15 fiberglass belted tires with white lettering.

Details: Front spoiler standard, unique, "hockey stick" striping, matte black hood, high-back bucket seats, carpeting, aluminum valve covers. Collapsible, space saver spare tire.

Colors: Grabber Blue, Grabber Green, Grabber Orange. Plus 8 other colors.

Options: Special 3.50 or 3.91 Traction-Lok rear axle. Rear deck spoiler. Sport Slats louvers to cover backlite. Power steering. Magnum 500 chrome wheels. AM or AM/FM Stereo Radio. 8000-rpm tachometer, console. Knitted vinyl trim. (Note air conditioning is not available on Boss 302.)

take-off, don't take our word for it, give it a try. We glue the Boss to the road on 15-inch wheels with hub cap trim rings, shod with F60 x 15 superwide fiberglass belted bias-ply tires. All this standard equipment leaves you little to option but the fun things—like Magnum 500 chrome wheels, and those great Sport Slats for the tinted backlite. That's Boss 302. Your only problem . . . deciding whether to drive it or "Trans-Am" it.

Paint a number on your Boss 302, put a big gas tank in it, and call yourself Parnelli Jones.

Mach 1-quickest pony of them all!

Mach I. Just one model—the fastback with built-in spoiler. You don't need any more, and neither did Mickey Thompson when he boomed the prototype across the endless Bonneville Salt Flats to shatter an armload of Class B and C records.

Obviously the big hit with the Mustang Mach I has always been the great choice of power, and that's just the way we're going to keep things. To start off, there's the standard 351 2V job . . . and for street work it's a bushy-tailed mill indeed. Then come the options. Exhibit A: one brand-new 351 4V V-8. This is the one with the "Cleveland" heads. It has huge (2.19" intakes, 1.71" exhausts), canted valves and a walloping 11.0:1 compression ratio. Power? Three hundred big, strong, born-and-bred-in-America horses.

Not bad for the first option . . . right? Next is the 428 4V Cobra. This puts 440 foot-pounds of torque where it will do the most good. If you really want to move out quick, you can have your Mach I with a 428 Cobra Jet. This giant jewel of an engine features the functional "Shaker" hood scoop. It shakes and so does the competition. Nice thing about the people who build the Mach I . . . they don't do half the job and then lay down their tools. No matter which engine you pick—and we know it's a tough decision—you get the competition suspension. This includes extra heavy-duty front and rear springs, extra heavy-duty shock absorbers, and front and rear stabilizer bars. Also you get fiberglass belted tires. All the power you need, plus a suspension that lets you get it to the road. That's what makes the Mach I a complete package. And for '70, the Mach I looks as good as it goes. There's a unique black grille with driving lamps, black or white hood paint, wide aluminum rocker panel trim, high-back buckets in knitted vinyl, full instrumentation, woodtoned applique on panel and console, sweep-hand electric clock, and more. Get yourself a Mach I 428 and really "shake up" the troops.

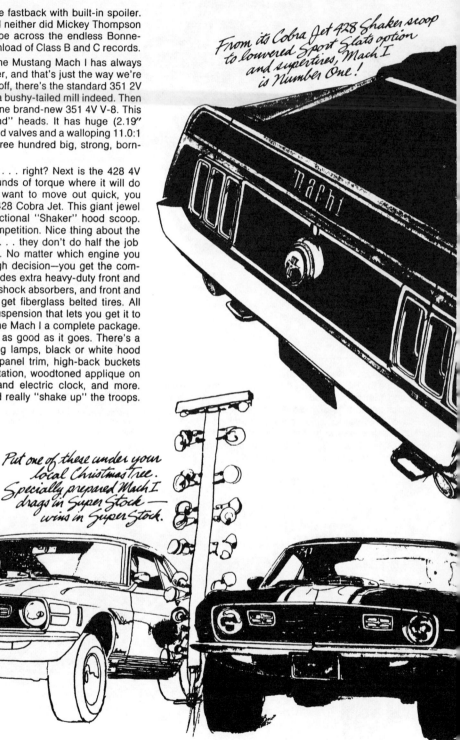

From its Cobra Jet 428 Shaker scoop to louvered Sport Slats option and supertires, Mach I is Number One!

Put one of these under your local Christmas tree. Specially prepared Mach I drags in Super Stock— wins in Super Stock.

Wheels: 14", 7" rim, F70 x 14 wide tread, fiberglass belted bias ply white sidewall tires (raised white letters with 428 CJ). **Suspension:** Competition type with front and rear stabilizer bar and extra heavy-duty springs, front shocks and rear shocks.

Details: Dual racing mirrors, high-back knitted vinyl bucket seats, console, sound package, three-spoke Rim-Blow woodtoned steering wheel, woodtoned appliques on instrument panel with clock, dual hood lock pins, rocker panel molding, honeycomb back panel applique, deck lid tape stripe, painted hood stripes, sports wheel covers, hood scoop (functional "Shaker" hood scoop on 428 4V Cobra Jet Ram-Air engine, optional with 351 2V and 4V V-8), unique grille with simulated driving lamps, pop-open gas cap, bright dual exhaust extensions with 351 4V and 428 4V engines.

Colors: Grabber Green, Grabber Blue, Grabber Orange, plus 13 other colors.

Mach 1 Options: Power Steering, AM or AM/FM Stereo Radio. Drag Pack (with 428 Cobra V-8), including Traction-Lok differential with 3.91 or 4.30 No-Spin differential, plus modified oil cooler, modified cap screw connecting rods, camshaft flywheel and damper. Quick ratio (16:1) manual steering, rear spoiler, sport slats for backlite. Tilt steering wheel, and much more.

Engines: Standard—351 CID 2V V-8. **Optional**—351 4V V-8, 428 Cobra 4V V-8, 428 Cobra Jet 4V Ram-Air V-8. (See back page for detailed engine specifications.) **Transmissions: Standard**—3-speed fully synchronized manual; ratios: 2.42:1, 1.61:1, 1.0:1. (3-speed not available with 428 CID V-8's.) **Optional**—4-speed fully synchronized manual with Hurst Shifter® (available with all engines); wide ratios: 2.78:1, 1.93:1, 1.36:1, 1.0:1, close ratios: 2.32:1, 1.69:1, 1.29:1, 1.0:1. (Note: 428 CID V-8's require close-ratio 4-speed.) SelectShift Cruise-O-Matic, ratios: 2.46:1, 1.46:1, 1.0:1. **Rear Axle:** Ratios: 3-speed manual, 2.75:1, 3.0, 3.25; 4-speed manual, 3.0, 3.25, 3.50. SelectShift, 2.75, 3.0, 3.25, 3.50. Traction-Lok, 3.0, 3.25, 3.50, 3.91. No-Spin (w/428 Cobra and CJ Ram-Air manual transmission) 4.30. **Brakes:** 10-in. drums, lining area 173.3 sq. in. **Optional**—Floating Caliper, Front Power Disc Brakes, swept area 231.0 sq. in. **Wheelbase:** 108.0". Length 187.4". Tread, front and rear 58.5".

Boss 429. An earth-shaking combination of big-bore engine and Trans-Am body. Limited production job, coax your dealer!

1971-1973

The 1971 Mustang's new look and substantially larger dimensions set it apart from earlier models. However, plenty of long-lived styling features were retained to maintain strong design continuity. For example, the grille once again carried the corralled mustang ornament with side horizontal bars. And while their form was altered for 1971, the triple lense arrangement of the taillights was continued. The Mustang's overall length was now 189.5 inches (up from 187.4 inches), width grew from 71.7 inches to 74.1 inches and, for the first time in its history, the Mustang's wheelbase was increased (from 108 inches to 109 inches).

Debuting in November, 1970, as the replacement for the Boss 302, was the Boss 351 which, like its predecessor, was technically an option for the SportsRoof model. This body style with its 50.1 inch height and long, sloping rear deck (the backlight was just 14 degrees from a horizontal position) was well suited to the Boss Mustang's image as a serious road machine. The dramatic slope of the roof tapered off to the rear deck lid, which carried a Boss 351 decal. Both the lower back panel and valance were painted (depending on which of the eleven available body colors were selected) either black or argent, as were the Boss 351's hood and body stripes. Both of these latter items were given a fresh new look for 1971. Twin NASA hood scoops were standard and large, circular twist locks were placed on the hood's forward surface. The grille features of the Boss 351 included twin rectangular-shaped foglights and the Mustang tricolor logo in its center. A front spoiler was included in the 351 package and either a body-colored or chrome-finished bumper was installed. Accentuating the low height of the Boss 351 body was a new form for its side stripes. Rising from the forward area of the front fender, they curved sharply back to run full body length with their pattern broken by the upper curves of the wheel arcs. Rounding out the Boss 351 exterior styling features was black or argent paint applied to the lower body section and a Boss 351 Mustang inscription behind the front fender wheel. Bright wheel rims and flat hub caps were standard for the Boss 351, but its F60-15 tires could be mounted on optional equipment Magnum 500 wheels with either an argent or chrome finish.

Exclusive to the Boss 351 was its engine, which was developed from the 302 V-8. Among its features were extruded aluminum pistons, mechanical lifters, canted valve train and a 750 cfm, four-barrel carburetor. Maximum horsepower was 330 at 5400 rpm and peak torque was 370 lb-ft at 4000 rpm. A 3.91:1 axle with a Traction-Lok differential was standard, as was a "competition suspension." A new dash panel with deeply recessed instruments was installed in all 1971 Mustangs. The circular speedometer with both kilometer and miles per hour readings, (a feature first used for the 1970 luxury model Grande Mustang) was to the steering column's right, with identically sized dial housing warning lights for oil pressure, engine temperature, alternator and brake system. Directly above the steering column was the smaller fuel gauge. A Special Instrumentation Group consisting of a trip odometer and gauges (mounted midway across the dash) for oil pressure, ampere output and engine temperature was standard on the Boss 351 and optional at $79 for other Mustangs.

While its standard engine was the 351 cid Windsor V-8 fitted with a two-barrel Motorcraft carburetor and rated at a modest 240 hp at 4600 rpm, the optional engine offering for the Mach I possessed the necessary muscle to create a high performing Mustang.

Reasonably priced at $180 was a 351 Cleveland V-8 with a four-barrel Holley, 10.7:1 compression ratio and 285 hp at 5400 rpm. The 370 hp, 429 cid Cobra Jet listed for $467. If Ram-Air was added to the 429 V-8 its price rose to $531. The ultimate Mach I engine choice was the 375 hp Super Cobra Jet, which was included in either of the two Drag Pack options, priced at $155 (3.91:1 Traction-Lok) and $207 (4.11:1 Detroit Locker). This engine featured four-bolt main bearings, mechanical lifters and a high lift cam.

The Mach I utilized the Boss 351 grille and lower body argent or black finish, body color front bumpers and hood locks. In addition a chrome strip bordered the region along with a special hood paint scheme (either black or argent) were applied. Also found on the base priced $3,268 Mach I were Mach I decals on the front fenders and rear deck and a black or argent insert for the lower back panel with a texture similar to that of the front grille. A pop-open gas cap was also supplied, along with striping along the rear deck lid. The Mach I interior was that of the standard SportsRoof version but for $130 a more elaborate Sports Interior was available.

Total model year production of all Mustangs was 149,678. Of this number, 36,449 were Mach I models. Precise output of Boss 351 versions is unknown, but Phil Hall in "Fearsome Fords 1959-73" reports that the total is estimated to slightly exceed 1,800 cars.

Nineteen seventy-two was the year the Mustang's performance machine wound down with rapidity. The Boss 351 model was eliminated and all 429 cid V-8s were dropped from the Mustang's optional engine list. Styling changes were of a very minor nature. A Mustang script was positioned above the right taillight and both the SportsRoof and Mach I models were fitted with the same grille consisting of twin spotlights and the familiar Mustang center emblem. This feature was also included in a new Exterior Decor Group option for other Mustang models.

Initial engine entrants in the Mustang's lineup, all of which were assigned SAE net horsepower ratings for the first time, began with the 250 cid six with a 99 hp output. The 302 cid V-8 offered 141 hp and the Windsor 351 cid V-8 was credited with a maximum 177 hp output. With a four-barrel carburetor and an 8.6:1 compression ratio, the 351 cid Cleveland V-8 delivered a strong 266 hp. While the Boss 351 was temporarily dead, its resurrection (a limited one, since only approximately 1,000 were turned out) took place in mid-season. Thus it was that the 351 HO (High Output) signaled the end of nearly 10 years of great Mustang engines. It brought the curtains down with class, providing 275 hp (net) at 6000 rpm and 286 ft-lb at 3800 rpm. The 351 HO contained virtually all the vital internal components of the Boss 351, such as its angled valves and forged pistons, although its compression ratio of 8.8:1 was pretty mild when stacked against the 11.2:1 of the Boss 351. This engine was available in all Mustang models for $894 as part of a fairly comprehensive performance package. Included under this price umbrella were power front disc brakes, competition suspension, F60-15, Firestone Wide Oval fiberglass tires on 7-inch wheels, four-speed wide-ratio manual transmission with 3.91:1 Traction Lok rear axle, plus a heavy-duty radiator and battery. When installed in a Mach I Mustang, this package's price was reduced to $865 since several components were included on the Mach I as standard equipment.

The base engine for the Mach I was the 302 V-8 with two-barrel carburetor, but all three versions of the 351 V-8 were optional. Along with the previously mentioned sports grille, the Mach I was equipped with the twin NASA scoop hood (a plain hood could be installed with the 302 V-8). Available for $24 for the Mach I as well as other Mustangs was a side trim option that was virtually identical to that of the 1971 Boss 351. Other performance options available for the Mach I included a rear spoiler ($24) and Magnum 500 chrome wheels ($143).

Ford offered two interesting 1972½ Sprint Decor options for the Hardtop and SportsRoof Mustangs. The Package A version, listing for $156, provided a white body with blue hood inserts and red accent stripes. Color-keyed hubcaps, white sidewall tires and dual racing-style mirrors were also included, as was a USA shield-type emblem on the rear fenders. The interior trim followed this patriotic theme with blue seat backs, white panels and red piping for the all-vinyl seats. The $347, Package B version added a competition suspension and raised white letter tires mounted on Magnum 500 chrome wheels.

Nineteen seventy-two was not a great sales-production year for the Mustang, with the records showing sales of 119,920 and a model year output of 125,093 cars.

With a new, dramatically downsized Mustang awaiting a 1974 model year introduction, the final version of the original Mustang styling-design philosophy was not radically changed from 1972. The most obvious appearance revisions included a new grille fitted with vertical parking lights (sport lamps were part of the $51 Decor Group option which was offered only on the base hardtop and convertible), with the mustang in its corral once again serving as a center ornament. The grille's gridwork was of an eggcrate pattern. Preparing the American consumer for the shape of headlights yet to come were the rectangular bezels for the single headlamps. Due to new federal bumper regulations, the front bumpers of body-colored urethane were repositioned further forward than previously and were connected to impact absorbing devices in the front body structure. This change extended the Mustang's overall length to 193.8 inches.

The most significant engineering refinement for 1973 involved the use of larger front shock absorbers with revised calibration. Their installation provided an additional 1/4 inch of front suspension travel and, according to Ford, improved rebound control, road feel and ride. Larger front drum brakes were installed on all Mustangs except the convertible, which had power front disc brakes as standard equipment. Mustangs with one of the available 351 cid V-8 engines were fitted with these brakes as a mandatory, $62.05 option.

New options for 1973 included steel belted radial tires, an improved electric rear window defroster listing for $57 (not available with the six cylinder engine or convertible), sports-type 14x6 forged aluminum wheels and a leather-wrapped steering wheel.

The Mach I Mustang was easily identified by its new wide side striping, which ran from the body region directly ahead of the front wheels to the leading edge of the rear wheel cutout and rear deck trim with large Mach I lettering above the right rear taillamp. The familiar honeycomb applique was placed in the lower back panel. Front end features unique to the Mach I were its grille center emblem, which consisted of the galloping mustang, tri-color vertical bar and blacked-out headlight bezels.

Included in the Mach I base price of $3,003 was the 302-2V (two-barrel carburetor) V-8 with ratings of 141 hp at 4000 rpm, 229 ft-lb of torque at 2600 rpm and an 8.0:1 compression ratio. The 351-2V V-8 was available for an additional $40.79 and delivered 173 hp at 4400 rpm and 258 ft-lb at 2400 rpm. Its compression ratio was also 8.0:1. The 351CJ with a four-barrel carburetor and modest 7.9:1 compression ratio was, depending on the source, capable of a maximum output of 246, 248, 259 or 264 hp.

Ford continued to offer a ram induction option which included the functional NASA hood scoops along with black or argent two-tone paint, hood lock pins and ram air engine decals. However it was available, at $58.24, only with the 351 cid V-8 with two-barrel carburetor. A non-functional version was standard on Mach I Mustangs with either version of the 351 engine. If desired, the 302 engined Mach I could also be ordered with a smooth hood with no change in price.

A Mach I Sports Interior Option, retailing for $115.44 and available for either the SportsRoof or Mach I, included knitted vinyl high-back bucket seats, gauges for oil pressure, engine temperature, ammeter, a tachometer and trip odometer. The dash featured a black instrument panel applique with a wood-tone center. Standard on the Mach I was an identification plate in the center of the panel.

Total production of all Mustangs was 134,867 of which 35,440 were Mach I models.

The Mustang catalogues grew substantially in physical size in 1971, 1972 and 1973 even as musclecar sales were rapidly evaporating. At the same time, the full-line Ford brochures became less and less impressive and the Mustang's place in them did, too. Excerpts from the 1971 Mustang catalogue appear on pages 68-71, while the Mustang panel from the full-line folder appears on pages 66-67. Excerpts from the 1972 Mustang catalogue appear on pages 72-73. A card on the mid-year Sprint is reproduced on page 74, and a "Special Spring Values" ad appears on page 75. Excerpts from the 1973 Mustang catalogue appear on pages 76-78.

'71 Mustang

America's challenge to the great European road cars.

Mustang '71 . . . six exciting new models with great European flair — American style, so you needn't be a wealthy Count or Countess to afford one. Every detail is crafted with care. And it shows. In looks. In roadability. In quicker, more precise handling.

Among Mustang's many fine standards are: thin-shell High Back bucket seats; DirectAire Ventilation for balanced air circulation; a new-style instrument panel; a new Mini-Console; Uni-Lock Harness (one buckle for shoulder and lap belts), and more.

Mach 1 — fantastico! (Shown on cover.) Dramatic new flatback styling with hood scoops, Color Keyed Spoiler-Bumper, competition suspension, belted wide ovals—all standard. So are dual racing mirrors and a 302 cube 2V V-8. New optional Mach 1 Sports Interior with knitted vinyl inserts and accent stripes on High Back buckets; electric clock; gauge cluster, and many others, make Mach 1 fantastic inside.

Mustang Grandé—elegante! The Mustang with Grandé manners presents a crisp, new roofline with vinyl roof, standard. Other standards: 3-speed synchronized manual transmission and 250 CID Six engine, Rich Lambeth

Mustang SportsRoof

Mustang Convertible

Mach 1 Sports Interior Option

Mustang Grandé Interior

cloth and vinyl bucket seat trim, electric clock, woodtone panel accents, wheel covers, dual racing mirrors, dual bodyside paint stripes.

SportsRoof, Hardtop, Convertible— wundercars!
All great American road cars. And no wonder. Five optional V-8 engines include a new 429 cube CJ-R V-8 with Ram-Air. Optional transmissions are SelectShift automatic transmission and the 4-Speed Manual with Hurst Shifter®. SportsRoof backlite is tinted. Convertible gives you a 5-ply vinyl, power-operated top with glass backlite, standard.

Boss 351 — blitz machine!
Standard 351 cube, 330-hp V-8, NASA-type functional hood scoops, competition suspension with staggered rear shocks, front spoiler, w-i-d-e F60-15 tires, and more.

New Steel Guard Rails
in side doors of *all* Mustangs provide a more solid wall for greater impact strength between you and the outside world.

Steel Guard Rails

And there's a host of options to help design your own Mustang. Attractions like: power from 351 CID 4V V-8 to a 429 CID 4V CJ-R, SelectAire Conditioner, AM/FM Stereo Radio, Vinyl Roof (Hardtop and SportsRoof), Magnum 500 Chrome Wheels, and more. Mustang: the exciting personal road car that's so easy to own.

Mustang measures up nicely with anything Europe offers.

Mustang Grandé

MACH I

Mach 1 '71 is a fantastic road car
you can only see coolly tooling down the Autostrada to Rome or the Autobahn to Munich. Right? Not quite. The all-new Mach 1 (illustrated previous page) is here, now, ready to move you over roads near and far in Mach-nificent style. Sure, the new roofline seems unreal. But it's as real and wild as Mach 1's new concealed windshield wipers and cowl air intakes, recessed door handles, color-keyed dual racing mirrors, and sporty wheel trim rings . . . all standard. Plus honeycomb grille, sport driving lamps and a dramatic Color Keyed Spoiler-Bumper. Standard hood style can be chosen with or without new NASA Type Hood Scoops (included with optional engines). Road-holding is a natural Mach 1 standard because of its wider stance, lower profile, competition suspension, and belted, bias-ply E70-14 white sidewall wide ovals. Mach 1 motion comes from a 302 cube 2V V-8 and four optional V-8's topped by the new 429 cube 4V CJ-R V-8 with Dual Ram Induction. Same extra-punch Dual Ram Induction package is available as an option on 351 V-8's and includes functional NASA Type Hood Scoops, black or argent painted hood, engine/CID decals, and hood locking pins. Bright dual exhaust extensions are included with 351 4V or larger V-8's, with or without Dual Ram Induction. For extra grip and go, choose F70 tires with raised white letters and 4-speed manual transmission with Hurst Shifter®. Colors? Mach 1's got 'em: Pewter, Grabber Yellow, Grabber Green Metallic, Grabber Blue, plus seven others. People-conscious standards include side door Steel Guard Rails and easier-to-use Uni-Lock Harness.

High Back bucket seats are new thin-shell design in wipe-clean, all-vinyl trim. Locking steering column helps protect against theft. 100% nylon carpeting is color-keyed. And, you can enjoy the good-looking sport of a standard new Mini-Console or an optional center console with integral electric clock and hinged arm rest stowage compartment.

New Mach 1 Sports Interior Option
includes: High Back bucket seats with knitted vinyl inserts and accent stripes; deluxe 2-spoke steering wheel with woodtone insert; electric clock (panel mounted); bright pedal pads; molded door trim panels with integral pull handles and armrests; color-keyed carpet runners; oil pressure, water temperature and ammeter gauges; rear seat ash tray; deluxe black and woodtone instrument panel appliques.
Mach 1. Fantastic in any language, on any road.

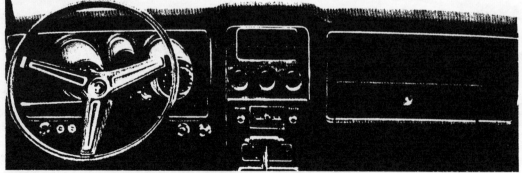

Better Idea Mach 1 Options include: tachometer & trip odometer, power side windows, SelectAire Conditioner, AM/FM Stereo Radio, power front disc brakes, Rim-Blow Deluxe 3-Spoke Steering Wheel, SelectShift Cruise-O-Matic transmission.

Mustang Specifications

Color and Trim: 16 Super Diamond Lustre Enamel exterior finishes (11 on Mach 1, Boss 351); 6 standard vinyl interior colors (5 in convertible); 6 knitted vinyl colors in Mach 1 Sports Interior Option and Convertible; 5 cloth/vinyl trims in Grandé; 2 knitted vinyl and 4 cloth/vinyl trims in Decor Group.

Engines*:

250 CID 1V Six—145 hp; 3.68" bore x 3.91" stroke; 9.0 to 1 comp. ratio; 7 main bearings; regular fuel.

302 CID 2V V-8—210 hp; 4.00" bore x 3.00" stroke; 9.0 to 1 comp. ratio; regular fuel.

351 CID 2V V-8—240 hp; 4.00" bore x 3.50" stroke; 9.0 to 1 comp. ratio; regular fuel.

351 CID 4V V-8—285 hp; 4.00" bore x 3.50" stroke; 10.7 to 1 comp. ratio; premium fuel.

351 CID 4V H.O. (Dual Ram Induction) V-8—330 hp; 4.00" bore x 3.00" stroke; 11.7 to 1 comp. ratio; premium fuel.

429 CID 4V CJ V-8—370 hp; 4.13" bore x 3.98" stroke; 11.3 to 1 comp. ratio; premium fuel.

429 CID 4V CJ-R (Dual Ram Induction) V-8 — 370 hp; 4.13" bore x 3.98" stroke; 11.3 to 1 comp. ratio; premium fuel.

*Hp ratings are gross hp derived from dynamometer.
**375 hp with Drag Pack option. Details page 15.

MODEL	STANDARD ENGINES	OPTIONAL V-8's
Hardtop, SportsRoof, Grandé, Convertible	250 1V Six (145 hp)	302 2V (210 hp) 351 2V (240 hp) 351 4V (285 hp) 429 4V CJ (370 hp**) 429 4V CJ-R (370 hp**)
Mach 1	302 2V V-8 (210 hp)	351 2V (240 hp) 351 4V (285 hp) 429 4V CJ (370 hp**) 429 4V CJ-R (370 hp**)
Boss 351	351 H.O. 4V V-8 (330 hp)	No optional engines available

Rear Axle: semi-floating hypoid type; permanently lubricated rear wheel bearings.

Front Suspension: angle-poised ball-joint type with coil springs; strut-stabilized lower arms; link-type stabilizer.

Rear Suspension: asymmetrical variable-rate design longitudinal 4-leaf springs. Diagonally mounted shocks.

ENGINES	TRANSMISSIONS			
	3-speed Floor-Mounted Manual	Select-Shift	4-speed Manual Wide-Ratio	4-speed Manual Close-Ratio
250 Six (145 hp)	X	X		
302 V-8 (210 hp)	X	X		
351 V-8 (240 hp)	X	X		
351 V-8 (285 hp)		X	X	
351 H.O. (330 hp)			X	
429 CJ V-8 (370 hp)		X		X
429 CJ-R (370 hp)		X		X

Engine Features: 6000-mile (or 6-month) maintenance schedule with full-flow disposable type oil filter; dry element air cleaner; auto. choke; self-adjusting valves with hydraulic lifters (mechanical lifters on Boss 351 and with Drag Pack Option); 12-volt electrical system; 38-amp. alternator with 250 Six, 42-amp. with 302 & 351 V-8's, 55-amp. with 429 & Boss 351 V-8's; 45 amp-hr battery with 250 Six and 302 & 351 2V V-8's, 55 amp-hr with 351 4V V-8, 80 amp-hr with Boss 351 & 429 V-8's.

Steering: recirculating ball-type, permanently lubricated. 27.7 to 1 overall ratio (22.1 to 1 power). Turning diameter 39.8 ft.

Brakes: dual hydraulic system with dual master cylinder. Self-adjusting, self-energizing design. Lining areas: 154.0 sq. in. (250 Six, 302 V-8); 173.3 sq. in. (351, 429); Boss 351, 231.0 sq. in. swept area.

Dimensions and Capacities: Length 189.5"; Width 74.1"; Height 50.8" (SportsRoof—50.1", Convertible—50.5"); Wheelbase 109"; Track—rear 61.0", front 61.5"; Trunk 9.5 cu. ft. (Hardtop), 8.3 cu. ft. (SportsRoof), 8.1 cu. ft. (Convertible). Fuel—20 gallons.

Weight: Hardtop—3087 lb.; SportsRoof—3057 lb.; Convertible 3209 lb.

NOTE: Your new 1971 Mustang comes equipped with factory engineered and approved parts such as the dependable Autolite Sta-Ful battery, Autolite Power-Tip spark plugs, Autolite shock absorbers, and an Autolite 6000-mile oil filter. Be sure to specify genuine Autolite parts whenever replacement is necessary.

While the information shown herein was correct when approved for printing, Ford Division reserves the right to discontinue or change at any time, specifications or designs without incurring any obligation. Some features shown or described are optional at extra cost.

Mustang Options. Your Designer Kits

Add your own special blend of luxury, convenience, performance, styling, with these better idea options. Your Mustang is designed to be designed by you.

Optional engines—all spirited V-8's. Select the eager 302 or 351 CID 2V's, or the new 351 4V. See back cover for engine/transmission specifications.

351-2V 302-2V 351-4V

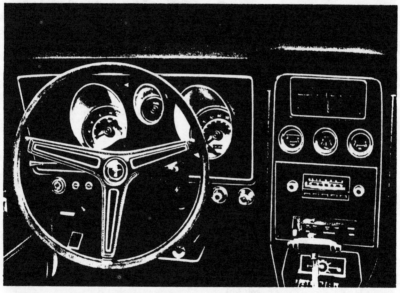

Rim-Blow 3-Spoke Steering Wheel lets you use horn without moving your hands from its woodtoned wheel rim. **Power Steering** gives you precise, immediate response for whatever the situation. It includes Vari-Ratio Steering on Mach I and models with optional competition suspension. The **Instrumentation Group** tells you what your V-8 is doing. It includes tachometer, trip odometer and oil pressure/ammeter/water temperature triple instrument pod. **Power Windows** with individual and master door-mounted controls, give you fingertip command of all side windows. **Center Floor Console** has integral electric clock and hinged armrest stowage compartment. It's perfectly suited for the **SelectShift Cruise-O-Matic Transmission** which lets you shift manually or automatically as you prefer. **AM/FM Stereo Radio** has two front speakers for proper stereo effect. Also available: **AM Radio** or **AM Radio with Stereosonic Tape System**. **SelectAire Conditioner** warms, cools, ventilates, defrosts. Tinted glass recommended. (Not available with 250 CID/3-speed manual combination.)

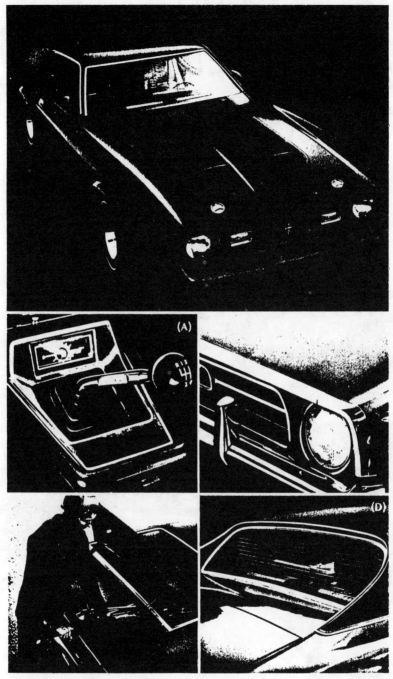

(A) 4-Speed Manual Transmission with Hurst Shifter® and linkage for fully synchronized sport shifting. It's available with the 351 4V engine.

(B) Sport Deck Rear Seat for Mach I and SportsRoof models includes rear seat that folds flat to form a carpeted deck and interior access to trunk. It's great for long or bulky items. Like skis as shown above.

(C) Protection Package guards your road machine against those hard-to-explain bumps and scrapes. It includes front and rear bumper guards and color-keyed vinyl insert bodyside molding.

(D) Rear Window Electric Defrost consists of thin conductive strips in the backlite which warm to help improve rear visibility. Available on Hardtop and SportsRoof.

1972

Put a little sprint in your life

Distinctive Cloth and
Vinyl Interior.
(Mustang Seats Shown)

Note: Pinto and Maverick shown here with optional
bright window frames and drip moldings.

RED WHITE AND SPRINTS

For Spring Only. A Mustang of a New Stripe.

A New Mustang Hardtop. It's a Special Spring Value at your Ford Dealer's. Now.

You take a classic Mustang Hardtop, right? (That practical, comfortable, stylish variety.) Add a sports-car hood—NASA-type scoops and all. Add dual racing mirrors. Color-keyed Spoiler bumper. A unique grille with sport lamps. Brighten the sides with Boss tape stripes. Oh yes, and wide tires with special trim rings. Then take a look at the special prices of the extras. You're home.

Spring won't last forever. Neither will these Special Spring Values at your Ford Dealer's. Now.

MUSTANG *Ford*

Mach 1 with black rear tape and paint treatment.

Ford Mustang Mach 1

New 1973 Mustang Mach 1 . . . smoothly rambunctious with marvelous road and ride manners . . . compliments of Mach 1's standard competition suspension system. Mach 1's wide, stable stance riding on Wide Oval white sidewalls makes beautiful waves and steady, balanced agility. You corner with excellent authority and deftly breeze SportsRoof-free with Mach 1's 302 CID 2V V-8 with smooth-working 3-speed, fully synchronized manual transmission or optional 3-speed Cruise-O-Matic transmission. The honeycomb texture black grille with new vertical sportlamp and new wide, sweeping bodyside and rear tape treatment are indisputably Mach 1. Standard NASA-styled hood scoops and color-keyed dual racing mirrors add sports car flavor for people who love sporty cars. Most important, Mach 1's tenacious loyalty on any road is deliberate, controlled, balanced. And Mach 1 can cut loose to whip you around mountains with super poise. Interior appointments confirm your image of sporty elegance. You get the Mustang's cockpit design,

exciting instrument panel, cushy bucket seats, all-vinyl interior, floor-mounted stick shift with Mini-console, ash tray, bonded door panels with armrests, deluxe 2-spoke steering wheel with woodtone insert, DirectAire Ventilation, lighter and glove box. Slip into an intense Mach 1 today. The anticipation couldn't possibly be as exciting as the reality.

MACH 1
SPORTS INTERIOR OPTION

The Mach 1 Sports Interior Option (shown here in Ginger) includes High Back bucket seats with knitted vinyl inserts and accent stripes, molded door trim panels with integral pull handles and armrests, bright pedal pads, color-accented carpet runners, plus a rear seat ash tray. The black applique, woodtone center Instrumentation Group included in the Sports Interior Option (also available with any V-8 equipped Mustang) includes a tachometer, trip odometer and triple pod oil pressure/water temperature/ammeter gauges. (Interior Color: GF.)

Mach 1 with tape stripe, blackout grille and molded color-keyed urethane front bumper.

STANDARD FEATURES: MACH 1

Mechanical: 302 CID 2V V-8 • 3-speed floor shift, fully synchronized manual transmission • new Energy Absorbing Bumper System • color-keyed urethane front bumper • competition suspension • choice of hood with or without NASA-styled hood scoops • E70 x 14 belted bias-ply WSW Wide Ovals.

Appearance and Comfort: color-keyed dual racing mirrors • color-keyed hood and fender moldings • honeycomb texture black grille with integral sportlamps • black rear panel applique • rear tape stripe with Mach 1 decal • wheel trim rings and hub caps • concealed windshield wipers • recessed exterior door handles • curved, ventless side glass • fixed rear quarter windows (except with optional power windows) • tinted glass backlite • DirectAire Ventilation • heater/defroster • all-vinyl seat trim • High Back buckets • bonded door trim panels with pull-type handles and armrests • Mini-console • color-keyed carpeting • courtesy dome light • deluxe two-spoke steering wheel with woodtone insert • lighter • reversible keys, "keyless" locking • Steel Guard Rails • Uni-Lock Shoulder/Lap Belts with Reminder System, plus all Ford Motor Company Lifeguard Design Safety Features listed on page 14.

SPECIFICATIONS: MUSTANG MACH 1

Wheelbase .... 109.0"
Length .... 193.8"
Width .... 74.1"
Height .... 50.0"
Track: rear .... 60.8"
       front .... 61.0"
Trunk Space .... 8.3 cu. ft.
Fuel Capacity and Grade, approx. .... 19.5 gal. (regular)
Curb Weight .... 3235 lb.

OPTIONS SHOWN

Deluxe Bumper Group, Wide Oval Black Sidewall Tires with Raised White Letters, Forged Aluminum Wheels, SelectShift Cruise-O-Matic, 351 4V V-8, SelectAire Conditioner, 2-Spoke Leather Wrapped Steering Wheel, Sport Interior Option, AM/FM Stereo Radio, Center Floor Console with Electric Clock and Hinged Armrest Stowage Compartment. See pages 10-13 for more extensive list of Mustang options. (License plate frames shown are Dealer accessory.)

FORD MUSTANG

Mustang Mach I (Color 5M)

Mustang Hardtop (Color 2B) with optional Full Wheel Covers, White Sidewalls.

There's Still Nothing Like It.

An experience in control and balance you'll always remember—that's the 1973 Ford Mustang. Satisfaction that comes from the ability to move, stop, turn and communicate with the pavement and with you.

Mustang expresses your own uniqueness. It's getup-and-go, sporty and luxury. Almost a decade ago, Mustang was designed to be designed by you. It still is. And there's still nothing like it!

Standard Power Team: Hardtop, SportsRoof, Convertible & Grandé—250 CID 1V Six with 3-speed full-sync manual transmission. **Mach I**—302 CID 2V V-8 with 3-speed full-sync manual transmission. **Optional Engines & Transmissions:** 302 CID 2V V-8, 351 CID 2V V-8, 351 CID 4V V-8, SelectShift Cruise-O-Matic, 4-Speed Manual with Hurst® Shifter.

Other Standard Features: Functional —DirectAire Ventilation • Heater/Defroster • Uni-Lock Shoulder/Lap Belts with Reminder System • Energy-Absorbing Bumper System • All Ford Motor Company Lifeguard Design Safety Features. **Appearance & Comfort**— Concealed Windshield Wipers • Color-Keyed Carpeting, and more. **Grandé**—Color-Keyed Dual Mirrors, Vinyl Roof, Deluxe Seat Trim, Bodyside Accent Stripes, Deluxe Wheel Covers,

Mustang's Standard Interior in White (Color AW) boasts sporty High Back Bucket Seats of handsome, durable all-vinyl, SelectShift.

Deluxe Instrument Panel, Electric Clock, High Back Buckets. **Mach I**— Competition Suspension, Dual Racing Mirrors, Integral Sportlamps, Side and Deck Lid Tape Stripes, Wheel Trim Rings/Hub Caps, All-Vinyl Seat Trim, High Back Buckets, White Sidewall Wide Oval Tires.

Specifications:	
Wheelbase	109.0"
Length	193.8"
Height	50.7"
Width	74.1"
Trunk	9.5 cu. ft.
Fuel Capacity & Type	19.5 gal. regular

Mustang Convertible (Color 4Q) with optional Full Wheel Covers, White Sidewalls.

Color codes indicated—example: (Color 6F) are in your Ford Dealer's 1973 Color and Trim Selections book. Ask to see it.

Full details are in the 1973 Ford Mustang Catalog available at your Ford Dealer's.

73 Ford Mustang

MODEL AVAILABILITY

Mustang Hardtop (Color 5A)

Mustang SportsRoof (Color 2B)

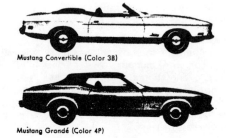

Mustang Convertible (Color 3B)

Mustang Grandé (Color 4P)

Just months short of a decade after the introduction of the first Mustang, Ford dramatically redefined the pony car concept and on, August 28, 1973, introduced the Mustang II. Physical comparisons between the Mustang II, the original Mustang and the 1973 model were startling:

	Mustang II	1964 1/2 Mustang	1973 Mustang
Wheelbase	96 inches	108 inches	109 inches
Overall length	175 inches	181.6 inches	193.8 inches
Width	70.2 inches	68.2 inches	74.1 inches
Height	49.9 inches	51.0 inches	50.7 inches

Further accentuating the Mustang II's departure from past practice was its engine lineup. A 2.3 liter four cylinder overhead engine was standard and the optional 2.8 liter, push-rod V-6 was manufactured in Cologne, Germany. In addition, the standard transmission for the Mustang II was a Ford-designed four-speed built by Borg-Warner. A rack and pinion steering system was employed that could also be power assisted. But Ford wasn't throwing the baby out with the wash water and incorporated plenty of styling cues into the appearance of the Mustang II linking it to earlier Mustangs. For example, the outline of the Mustang II's side body indentation followed a very familiar form, as did the simple eggcrate grille and galloping pony emblem.

The Mustang II also continued to keep the Mach I tradition alive. The standard Mach I model was based upon the hatchback, 2+2 version and was priced at $3,674. Its standard V-6 engine with dual exhausts, two-barrel Holley-Weber carburetor and 8.2:1 compression ratio developed 119 hp at 5200 rpm and 147 ft-lb at 2800 rpm.

The Mach I's standard suspension, like that of all Mustang II models, consisted of unequal length control arms up front with the coil spring mounted on the lower arm. The entire system was assembled onto a rubber-mounted subframe. At the rear, leaf springs two inches longer than the Pinto's were used with staggered tubular shocks. Included in the optional $133 Rallye Package was a competition suspension which provided a 0.95 inch front anti-roll bar in place of the standard 0.75 inch unit, stiffer springs, Gabriel adjustable shock absorbers and a 0.69 inch anti-roll bar at the rear. Standard tires for the Mach I were BR70-13 radials on styled steel wheels, but wider CR70-13 tires on five inch alloy wheels were available.

The Mach I interior with its standard 0-6000 rpm tachometer could be fitted with the $96 Ghia or Luxury Interior Group option, which featured patterned vinyl upholstery (color-coordinated to the exterior finish), with accent strips on the seats and backrest, simulated wood inserts on door panels, larger arm rests and 25-ounce cut-pile carpeting.

Although the Mid-East oil embargo and the increasing rate of inflation had a negative impact on sales midway through the model year, Mustang II production nevertheless was an impressive: 385,993, of which 44,046 were Mach I models.

Exterior appearance changes for 1975 were kept to a minimum. A larger eggcrate insert for the grille was used and instead of being recessed, as in 1974, it was now nearly flush with the grille outline. The major performance news centered around the availability of 133 hp, 302 cid V-8s with a two-barrel Motorcraft carburetor and 8.0:1 compression ratio as an option for any Mustang II. When installed in a Mach I, this V-8 and three-speed SelectShift Cruise-O-Matic (no manual gearbox was available with the V-8) added $203 to the Mach I's base price of $4,188. Also included in this package was the Extended Range Fuel Tank with a total capacity of 16.5 gallons, up 3.5 gallons from the standard tank's volume.

Model year production fell dramatically to 188,575. Output of Mach I models totalled 21,062 cars.

The most important performance development for 1976 was the availability of a four-speed manual transmission for the 302 cid V-8. However a flash from the past in the form of a Cobra II option package suggested, despite of its standard 2300 cc four cylinder engine, that Ford still recognized the style if not the substance of the Mustang's performance history. Exterior features of the Cobra II consisted of racing stripes (combinations of blue, red or green on white plus gold on black, as well as white stripes on a bright blue metallic body, were eventually offered), a blackout grille, dual racing mirrors, rear window louvers, front air dam, non-functional hood scoop plus Cobra insignias on the front fenders, grille, rear spoiler and wheel centers.

Along with the other Mustang II models, the Cobra II interior had its windshield wiper controls mounted on a steering column stalk (this feature had been adopted mid-way through the 1975 model year) and full instrumentation, including tachometer, fuel level, ammeter and engine coolant temperature gauges. In addition, full length armrests were installed along with an engine-turned applique on the instrument panel and door panels.

A second pseudo-performance Stallion group option was offered for either the three-door or two-door Hardtop models. Key elements consisted of a blackout grille, black window moldings, wiper arms and lower body section, styled steel wheels and Stallion side body decals. If desired, this option could be linked to the MPG feature which combined the 2300 cc four cylinder engine with a 3.18:1 rear axle ratio.

Model year production for 1976 dropped slightly from 1975's level to 187,567 units.

With problems of air pollution, government certifications and miles-per-gallon ratings paramount in Detroit's view, the Mustang II was virtually unchanged for the 1977 model year. The base price of the Mach I with the standard 2800 cc four cylinder engine was $4,332, with the optional 302 cid V-8 adding an additional $48. The surprisingly popular Cobra II package (now available in new red or green on white body color combinations) was again offered for $514 (above the base price of $3,901 for the 2+2 model), as were the Rallye and Sports Performance Packages. Their prices varied with the model on which they were installed. For example, when ordered for the Mach I, the Sports Performance Package retailed for only $51. However, the price rose to $320 when ordered for a 2+2 with the Cobra II options and to $397 when specified for a Ghia luxury model Mustang II. The principal features of the Sports Performance Package included the 302 V-8, heavy-duty four-speed manual transmission, power steering and brakes and, for the Mach I, 195R/70 black wall tires with white letters. The Rallye Package (priced at $54 for Mach I and Cobra II equipped Mustangs and $101 for all others) featured a heavy-duty cooling system, stiffer springs, adjustable shocks, rear stabilizer bar and the remote control dual, color-keyed sport mirrors that were standard on the Mach I and Cobra II. Adding to the appeal of all hatchback Mustangs and especially that of the Cobra II or Mach I was the new $750 T-Top feature supplied to Ford by the American Sunroof Corporation.

Model year production declined to 153,173.

Although there were only minimal styling changes for 1978, the Mustang II ended its five year tour of duty on an upbeat note clearly indicating that the Mustang's future contained high performance models. A Fashion Accessory Package with bodyside pinstripes that Ford said was designed for its female customers definitely didn't fall into that category, but the Cobra II's new stablemate, the King Cobra, surely did. A very large front end dam which extended into the front wheel wells was pinstriped, as were the side window surrounds. The rear spoiler carried a wide stripe with King Cobra lettering positioned above the right side taillights. What Ford described as a "rear quarter flair" gave the King Cobra the impression of being equipped with a sturdy roll bar. Additional body trim features included blacked out headlight bezels, grille and grille molding, King Cobra lettering on the side door panels, a 5.0 label on the hood scoop (the 5 liter, 302 cid, V-8 was standard) and a stylized Cobra decal for the front hood surface.

Assisting the V-8 engine in substantiating the performance image of the King Cobra was a four-speed manual gearbox, power front disc brakes, heavy-duty springs and adjustable shock absorbers.

Giving the Cobra II a fresh for '78 appearance were wide tricolor stripes that ran full body length, plus new body side striping (also tricolor) incorporating Cobra lettering into its design.

Although they were both well off the records of 1974, the 1978 model production and sales of 192,410 and 179,039 respectively, represented substantial improvements over the levels of 1977.

The 1974-1978 catalogues were, in general, a bit smaller than their immediate predecessors. The 1974 Mustangs represented the most important news since 1964 and this was trumpeted in a couple of ads (see pages 81-83). The 1974 Mustang catalogue is excerpted (see pages 84-85). The Mustang panel from the 1975 full-line Ford catalogue appears on page 86 and an excerpt from the 1975 Mustang catalogue appears on page 87. A magazine ad for the 1976 Cobra II is reproduced on pages 88-89. Mustang material from the 1977 "Free Wheelin'" catalogue appears on pages 90-91. Excerpts from the 1977 Mustang catalogue appear on pages 92-95. Excerpts from the 1978 Mustang catalogue appear on pages 96-100.

It just may be the best news from Detroit in 9½ years.

One thing's for sure. We don't have to tell you what the original Mustang started when it was introduced 9½ years ago.

It was much more than a new car. It was a revolutionary idea: performance in a small package.

This year, the new Mach 1 is that same, special kind of car. On today's kind of terms.

Size.
First of all (and probably most obvious of all), it's smaller. A bit smaller than the original Mustang of 9½ years ago and more than 18 inches shorter than last year's model. And with a lot less weight to carry, Mustang II is an extremely nimble car.

A special engine for a special car. Standard.
Open the hood of a new Mach 1 and you'll see something different for an American-built production car: a V-6 engine that measures a very respectable 2.8 liters. Its short stroke tells you this is one new engine

that's no stranger to the big numbers on the tach.

With it you get the performance you want—without becoming the best customer at your neighborhood service station.

There's still more. And that's standard too.
In the car: Mach 1 gives you an instrument panel with true gauges. Accurate gauges plus a large cluster of warning lights to keep you in charge. And get this, even a tach is standard.

Of course, you'd expect a 4-speed transmission in a car like this. And this one features top rail shifting. A design that does away with external shifters and linkage rods. It's solid, smooth and quick.

And there's more. Like rack-and-pinion steering (a plus in a performance car like this). And even creature comforts like full carpeting, European-type armrests and contoured front buckets.

Under the car: The '74 Mach 1 features a totally new suspension system. It's rubber-buffered and designed to absorb distracting

vibrations, but firm enough to keep you in close touch with the road. A front anti-sway bar is standard for ease of handling and control on curves. Also standard is a new sub-frame that helps reduce engine vibration as well as the jolts and jars of front-wheel road shocks. Staggered rear shocks help keep you in control during hard braking and fast acceleration. Radial tires and front disc brakes are included, too. (Are there any other kind?)

On the car: A machine that feels different should look different. So we gave the Mach 1 a special paint treatment with blacked-out rear deck and lower body. Dual racing mirrors and styled steel wheels are also standard.

Get ready for the options.
With all that we've just been through, there are still a few ways left to make a Mach 1 look and handle even better. Here goes:
Traction-lok differential.
CR70 Steel-belted radial raised white letter tires.
Competition suspension that gives you heavy-duty springs, adjustable shock absorbers, rear anti-sway bar.
Digital clock.
Leather-wrapped steering wheel.
A Rallye Package that includes all the above, plus an extra cooling package and sport exhaust with bright tips.
Anti-theft alarm system.
AM/FM Stereo with tape player.
Forged aluminum wheels.

Finally.
The Mach 1 is just one of 4 new Mustang II models. There's the elegant Ghia (shown below), classic two-door hardtop, sporty three-door 2 + 2 with convenient, fold-down rear seat.

They're all at your Ford dealer now.

Mach 1 shown is equipped with optional Forged Aluminum Wheels, Vinyl Insert Bodyside Moldings, Air Conditioning, AM/FM Stereo with tape player, Flipper Rear Windows, Luxury Interior and Rallye Package.

FORD MUSTANG II
FORD DIVISION (Ford)

Ford Mustang II Mach 1. The fun way to go First Class.

One look delivers the message. A message of excitement, performance and fun. The styling sets the tone. With sporty 3-door design, styled steel wheels with trim rings and dual color-keyed remote controlled mirrors. Black paint treatment at the lower bodysides and steel-belted radials with raised white letters label Mach 1 as a car of action. The Mustang II tachometer and separate ammeter, fuel and temperature gauges help you keep a ready eye on the engine. Contoured vinyl bucket seats with full-width headrests and sporty European-type armrests set the stage for action. And a smooth shifting 4-speed manual floor-mounted gearbox together with a new 2.8 Liter V-6 engine provide a power team to really move out ahead.

On the straightaway and through the hairpins, Mach 1 handles like it looks. Smooth. New rack-and-pinion steering (the kind expensive road cars use) helps glide it through the turns. The new isolated front sub-frame and the entire suspension system work together to give easy handling, positive control and a smooth ride.

Mustang II offers a broad list of options. For looks you can choose the sporty leather-wrapped steering wheel, bright electric paints, and a Luxury Interior Group.

For ride and handling, go with the competition suspension, power brakes or Rallye Package. See pages 16 through 19 for a complete list of options. And see the exciting Mach 1 for the driving experience of 1974.

NOTABLE STANDARD FEATURES--Mach 1

Functional: 2.8 Liter V-6 engine □ Fully synchronized 4-speed manual floor-mounted transmission □ Rack-and-pinion steering □ Manual front disc brakes □ 3-color taillights □ Tachometer □ Fuel, ammeter and temperature gauges □ Dual remote control color-keyed mirrors □ Fold-down rear seat □ Steel-belted radial ply raised white letter tires □ Impact Resistant Front and Rear Bumper Systems □ Seat Belt Interlock System □ Isolated front sub-frame □ All Ford Motor Company Lifeguard Design Safety Features on page 20.

Note: See Notable Standard Features above. Other items shown are optional.

The bright oval grille blends smoothly into the distinctive styling and trim of the exciting Mach 1. Bright Red (Code 2B).

The dramatic 3-door styling of the Mach 1 is accented by the sporty black lower bodyside paint all around and bold Mach 1 lettering. Medium Lime Yellow (Code 4W). Raised white letter steel-belted radial ply tires are standard on Mach 1.

Appearance and Comfort: Color-keyed, urethane-coated front and rear bumpers □ Bright windshield, backlite, drip, belt and center pillar moldings □ Styled steel wheels with chrome trim rings □ Black lower bodyside paint treatment □ Low-back bucket seats with full-width headrests □ Color-keyed cut-pile carpeting □ Vinyl door trim panels with European type armrests and integral pull handles □ Soft vinyl headlining □ Deluxe instrument panel □ Reversible keys, "keyless" locking.

MEASUREMENTS – Refer to 3-Door models on page 8.

Note: See Color Code reference on page 3.

MUSTANG II
Our small, sporty personal car.

Quiet-riding Mustang II Ghia. New higher level of luxury for 1975. Standard features include vinyl roof (half or full), new opera windows, spoke-style wheel covers, Ghia ornamentation and more! Dark Brown Metallic (Code 5Q).

This luxuriously tailored Cranberry interior (Code FH) completes the Silver Ghia Luxury Group. Meticulously trimmed in crushed velour Media upholstery. Handy center console included.

Presenting the new Silver Ghia Luxury Group. Exterior appointments include a brilliant Silver Metallic finish (Code 1G), Silver Normande grain half-vinyl roof with matching bodyside molding, Cranberry taping and unique hood ornament. Manually operated Glass Moonroof optional.

Last year's success car has done it again for 1975. Mustang II is more exciting than ever! With an even more impressive list of standard features, including steel-belted radial ply tires and solid state ignition. With an even wider choice of options, highlighted by the luxurious new Ghia Silver Luxury Group and a spirited new 302 CID V-8.

Choose from four distinctive models: Hardtop and Ghia with formal roofline, or the fastback-styled 2+2 and Mach 1 models. Mustang II's interiors are unbelievably luxurious and personal for a small car. Standard power team is a thrifty 2.3 Liter engine matched with a 4-speed manual floorshift. Besides the new optional V-8 (available exclusively with SelectShift Cruise-O-Matic), you can also select a 2.8 Liter V-6 with manual 4-speed. Test-drive Mustang II soon. It's more than a car . . . it's a feeling!

NOTABLE STANDARD FEATURES—MUSTANG II

Functional: 2.3 Liter 4-cylinder Engine with Solid State Ignition (2.8 Liter V-6, Mach 1) □ Floor-mounted 4-speed transmission □ Manual rack-and-pinion steering □ Manual front disc brakes □ 3-color taillights □ Fold-down rear seat & liftgate (2+2, Mach 1) □ Steel-belted radial ply BSW tires (Ghia WSW, Mach 1 RWL) □ Tachometer, fuel, ammeter and temperature gauges □ All Ford Lifeguard Design Safety Features.

Appearance & Comfort: Low-back bucket seats w/full width headrests □ European-type armrests □ Burled walnut woodtone dash appliques □ Bright window & wheel lip moldings □ Cut-pile carpeting □ Color-keyed urethane-covered bumpers □ Vinyl roof (Ghia) □ Wheel covers (Hardtop); styled steel wheels (2+2); styled steel wheels and trim rings (Mach 1); spoke-style wheel covers (Ghia).

Model Selector

Mustang II Hardtop—Pastel Blue (3Q)

Mustang II 3-Door 2+2—Bright Yellow (6E)

Mustang II Mach 1—Dark Red (2M)

Mustang II Ghia—Dark Brown Metallic (5Q)

MEASUREMENTS—Hardtop:	2-Door	3-Door
Wheelbase	96.2″	96.2″
Length	175.0″	175.0″
Height	50.0″	49.7″
Width	70.2″	70.2″
Usable Luggage Capacity (cu. ft.)	6.7	28.1*
Fuel Capacity (gal.) & Type—unleaded	13.0	13.0
Passenger Capacity	4	4
*Cargo Vol. index with rear seat down.		

Note: See Notable Standard Features above. Other items shown are optional.

Mustang II 3-Door 2+2.
Winning combination—practicality plus personal luxury.

2+2 combines sporty good looks and luxury with some of the practical space and convenience of a station wagon. Its big rear door swings up easily like a cargo hatch. A fold-down rear seat makes room for a cargo volume index of 28.1 cu. ft. Fastback lines, full wheel lip moldings, styled steel wheels and steel-belted radials—standard—add sporty flair.

Inside, you relax on deep-cushioned, comfortable bucket seats. All-vinyl trim, woodtone applique accents, full instrumentation lend a sporty note. And you ride quietly. Nimble handling, with surprising quickness, stems from a thrifty 2.3 Liter engine. More spirited go, economically, can be yours with the optional 2.8 Liter V-6 with 4-speed manual, or 302 CID 2V V-8 with SelectShift.

2+2. Practical luxury blend. With 3-door convenience and versatility. And for less than you probably expected to spend.

Practical 2+2 (right), with handy rear door and fold-down rear seat, in Medium Copper Metallic (Code 5M), plus styled steel wheels and optional trim rings.

Mach 1 in Bright Red (Code 2B). Racy styling says driving fun starts here. An authoritative 2.8 Liter V-6, plus 4-speed manual to back it up. What are you waiting for?

Mustang II Mach 1. Rediscover driving fun.

Look at Mach 1's racy lines and you might never guess its budget-stretching ways. Mach 1 has sporty touches like trim rings with styled steel wheels. Raised white letter steel-belted radials. Dramatic Black at the lower bodyside . . . lower bumpers . . . deck lid. Even Black at the paint break moldings. And useful color-keyed dual remote mirrors. All standard.

At the inside controls—the tachometer plus ammeter, fuel and temperature gauges help you keep an eagle eye on performance. Cushioned vinyl buckets, contoured for maximum support and comfort, have full-width headrests and European-type padded armrests. (See pages 6 and 7.)

A lively, fuel-conserving 2.8 Liter V-6 engine with solid state ignition is standard. So is a 4-speed manual transmission. A livelier, yet economical, 302 CID 2V V-8 is optional with SelectShift automatic transmission. You can add power front disc brakes, power rack-and-pinion steering, and more. Mach 1 looks solid and is solid. With a firm road feel. A nice blend of performance with comfort.

Rediscover driving fun with an exhilarating Mach 1 test drive. At your Ford Dealer's. And soon.

In 1966, a Texan named Carroll Shelby (far right) introduced his infamous Mustang Cobra (right). In a word: overpowering. Based on Mustang's solid roadability, the Shelby Cobra included refinements that made it a road racing champion.

Now in 1976, please welcome Cobra II (above). Ford's Mustang II 2 + 2 wrapped in an option package that does justice to the Cobra name.

Cobra II starts with 1976 Mustang standards like rack and pinion steering and front disc brakes. Then, bold racing stripes, blackout grille, racing mirrors, rear quarter window louvers, front air dam, rear decklid spoiler, engine-turned dash and door appliques and Cobra insignia all are added.

Underneath, BR70 steel-belted radials mounted on styled steel wheels with trim rings.

Cobra II. With the look and feel of the legendary Cobra. But designed to be more affordable.

Find out more about these fancied-up, free wheelin' Fords.

Ask about our free 24 page book, "Free Wheelin'," from your Ford Dealer.

FREE WHEELIN'

The closer you look, the better we look.

FORD MUSTANG II

FORD DIVISION

Ford Mustang II for 1977.
Sweet-handling SuperCoupe.

Everyone's got a favorite stretch of road. One that winds through the countryside with sweeping bends and corners that require just that little extra concentration. Mustang II is going to make that special bit of road even more interesting in 1977. That's because this year Mustang II is more responsive...so responsive, in fact, that our new carburetor linkage seems to be directly connected to an overhead cam, four-cylinder engine that's tough

to hold back. If you want even more excitement, there's a compact, lightweight optional 2.8 liter V-6, perfected in Europe, or a very strong optional 302-cubic-inch V-8.

Behind these quick, efficient power plants are two smooth transmissions. A slick do-it-yourself four-speed, and a crisp optional three-speed Select-Shift that does it for you. Both are mounted on the floor right next to your throttle leg. And be sure to give the SelectShift a try

before you decide. It's put together very much with the driver in mind. It not only shifts for itself, you can override the machinery and shift for *yourself*. Another must-try option is the four-way manual driver's seat. It goes back and forth, *plus* up and down. It's got a position that's just right to keep you in touch with the road *and* all those gauges keeping track of amps, temperature, rpm's, fuel and speed. Other things that make

Mustang II Mach 1

Customized Mustang II Hardtop

Mustang II very much a driver's car are rack and pinion steering, front disc brakes, staggered rear shocks, link-type stabilizer bars, close-ratio four-speed gearbox, and low-friction gearshift linkage. Put them all together and they spell Mustang II...a machine that handles with great snap and precision.

Once you've decided on Mustang II, your decisions have just begun. Mustang II's sweet handling comes in five packages. There's the hardtop... sweet handling at a low price. Next, the sleek

2 + 2 gives you a functional fold-down rear seat and wide-opening hatchback for easy loading. Then there's the Mach 1 and its striking cousin: Cobra II. Both with slippery looks to match their smooth performance. And finally, the most stylish of the five—the Ghia. If you're a driver you'll love Mustang II. If you're not, there's no better way to learn what driving's all about.

Is that it? Hardly. Because Mustang II is a car that invites customizing. Wild paint, wheels and tires, special equipment...whatever you have in mind. Come in and try a Mustang II today.

ENGINE SPECIFICATIONS

Cylinders	4 In-Line	V-6*	V-8
Displacement	2.3 Liter (140 cu. in.)	2.8 Liter (170.8 cu. in.)	302 cu. in.
Bore	3.78"	3.66"	4.00"
Stroke	3.126"	2.70"	3.00"
Carburetion	2-Barrel	2-Barrel†	2-Barrel
Valve Lifters	Hydraulic	Mechanical	Hydraulic

TRANSMISSIONS/REAR AXLE RATIOS

	4-Speed Manual	SelectShift Auto.
4-Cylinder	3.18	3.18
V-6	3.00	3.00
V-8	3.00*‡	3.00

DIMENSIONS

	Hardtop	2 + 2
Wheelbase	96.2"	96.2"
Overall Length	175.0"	175.0"
Overall Height	50.3"	50.0"
Overall Width	70.2"	70.2"
Tread, Front	55.6"	55.6"
Tread, Rear	55.8"	55.8"
Trunk or Cargo Vol. (cu. ft.)	6.7	22.8
Fuel Capacity (gal.) w/302 V-8	16.5	16.5
Curb Weight (lbs.) Base Vehicle	2,716	2,765

*Not available in high altitude areas.
†Variable venturi in Calif.   ‡Not available in Calif.

Mustang II Cobra II

Ford Mustang II. Go as sporty as you like.

(B) Mustang II Mach 1

(A) Cobra II. Runaway sales success.

(left) Combine flair with fun by choosing the new Cobra II Package option. Cobra II is available on the 4-passenger 2+2's shown in Polar White (Code 9D), with brilliant Red, Blue or Green racing stripes, or in Black (Code 1C), with Gold stripes.

You get these exterior features: front/rear deck spoilers □ Black louvered backlite and flipper quarter windows □ tricolor racing stripes on spoilers, hood, hood scoop, roof, rear deck, lower bodyside panels □ Cobra II emblem on Blackout grille with bright surround molding □ Black dual sport mirrors □ Cobra II bodyside identification □ styled steel wheels with trim rings □ raised white letter radials □ Black windshield wiper arms and windshield/backlite moldings.

The 2.3 liter engine and 4-speed manual transmission with floor shift are standard. More spirited action can be yours with 2.8 liter V-6† (2.8 VV in Calif.) or 302 CID 2V V-8 (302 VV in Calif.). SelectShift automatic transmission is available.

Inside Cobra II you get 2+2 standards like: brushed aluminum instrument panel applique □ tachometer, ammeter, temperature gauges □ Sport steering wheel □ low-back bucket seats, all-vinyl trim □ color-keyed carpeting □ fold-down rear seat, carpeted cargo area, and more. Plus: brushed aluminum door trim inserts, Cobra II nameplates.

(B) Exhilarating Mach 1.

(above) You see it here in Orange (Code 8G) with: Black lower bodyside/back panel/tape treatment □ dual sport mirrors □ bright lower bodyside molding □ Mach 1 insignia □ styled steel wheels with trim rings □ raised white letter

(C) 2+2 with Rallye Appearance Package.

(D) 2+2 with Appearance Decor Group.

radials. Under the racy lines churns a 2.8 liter 2V V-6† with 4-speed manual transmission and floor-mounted shift. All standard.

(C) 2+2 with Rallye Appearance Package. Tasteful, upbeat optional styling—in Black (Code 1C shown), or Polar White. Exterior excitements are: dual Gold-color bodyside/hood stripes □ Black moldings, door handles, lock □ Black antenna (when Ford radio ordered) □ Black wiper arms □ Black front spoiler □ Black grille and Gold-color surround molding □ Black dual sport mirrors □ dual Gold accents on bumper rub strips □ taillamp Gold surround accents □ Argent-styled steel wheels with trim rings. Striking interior items feature: choice of Black or White vinyl seats with Gold ribbed velour Touraine Cloth inserts, Gold welting □ Gold-color door panel

moldings. Carpeting and other components, color-keyed to Black or White exterior, add an impressive designer touch.

(D) 2+2 with Appearance Decor Group. (above) Now you can add spicy Tu-Tone paint ideas. The Appearance Group option shown in Polar White with Bright Red (Codes 9D, 2R), is also available in Polar White with Bright Aqua Glow (Code 7H), and Creme with Golden Glow (Codes 6P, 6V).

This option group includes dual accent tape stripes □ trim rings □ choice of all-vinyl or cloth/vinyl seat trim □ brushed aluminum instrument panel appliques. Wheel lip moldings are deleted.

†N.A. on high altitude area cars.

Note: See Notable Standard Features list, measurements and color code reference on back cover. Some items shown are optional, such as dual sport mirrors, White painted lacy spoke aluminum wheels, forged aluminum wheels, and front/rear bumper guards.

FORD MUSTANG II
2+2

(A) Mustang II 2+2 with T-Roof Convertible

Styling that makes the sky your limit.

(A) Mustang II with T-Roof Convertible. It will suit you to a "T"! The optional "T-Roof," which was so well received when it was introduced last year, is again available on all 3-door models (including 2+2, Mach 1, Cobra II and King Cobra). Shown with optional Rallye Appearance Package and in White (Code 9D), the "T-Roof" has the advantages of a convertible, yet it still retains the advantages of a hardtop. It features twin glass panels with a wide vinyl-inserted "roof band." Smoke-tinted, tempered safety glass panels can be easily removed in a matter of seconds. Vinyl pouches are provided for convenient trunk storage.

The "T-Roof." It makes the sky your limit, the moon and stars your ceiling, and the sun drops by most every day, thanks to still yet another better idea from Ford. See page 10 to see "T-Roof" panels in place.

(B) Mach 1. For the greatest getaway under the sun. If you're the type that wants extra power and performance, then Mach 1 is your answer. A standard 2.8 litre 2V V-6 engine makes Mach 1 a most spirited performer. Spirited for quicker pickup and greater passing ease. Spirited for that great getaway. And Mach 1 is just as easy on the eyes as it is on the road. That's because the Mach 1 has raised white letter steel-belted radials, 4-speed manual transmission, dual sport mirrors, black lower bodyside/back panel/tape treatment, four White-painted styled steel wheels with trim rings, bright lower body side molding, and Mach 1 insignia . . . all standard. See back cover for full list. Shown here in Bright Yellow (Code 6E), the Mach 1 is a most powerful and exhilarating way to go.

(C) The Rallye Appearance Package. If you're a man of distinction, then this highly popular optional package is for you. Bold and strikingly attractive, it features dual Gold color bodyside/hood stripes ☐ Black moldings ☐ Black door handles and lock ☐ Black antenna (when Ford radio is ordered) ☐ Black wiper arms ☐ Black front spoiler ☐ Gold grille and Gold-color taillights surround molding ☐ Black dual sport mirrors ☐ dual Gold accents on bumper rub strips ☐ four White styled steel wheels with trim rings. Up-tempo interior items include a choice of Black or White vinyl seats with Gold-ribbed velour Touraine Cloth inserts ☐ Non-leather wrapped Sport Steering Wheel ☐ Gold welting and Gold-color door panel moldings ☐ Color-keyed carpeting and other components add an impressive design touch. Mustang II 2+2 . . . a car you'll really want to rally around this year!

See your Ford Dealer soon for the thrill of driving Mustang II 2+2 and Mach 1. Once you do you're bound to be sold.

Note: See Notable Standard Features, Measurements and Color Code References on back cover.

Some items shown are optional, such as bumper guards, four styled steel wheels with trim rings, T-Roof Convertible, and white sidewall tires.

(B) Mustang II Mach 1

(C) Mustang II 2 + 2 with Rallye Appearance Package

FORD MUSTANG II
KING COBRA/COBRA II

(A) Mustang II King Cobra

You've got an audience with the King.

(A) King Cobra. The new King of the road! Presenting . . . the King Cobra. Unmistakably bold. The ultimate in flair. A car designed to rule its class.

Experience the way King Cobra exuberantly merges in traffic. Enjoy its superb ride and handling. The way it corners and hugs the road. And check out all the features of the King Cobra option. Features like: □ Unique tape treatment, pinstriping on all major areas, words "King Cobra" on sides and rear decklid spoiler □ Distinctive hood scoop with emblem □ Unique front air dam □ Color-keyed dual sport mirrors □ Rear quarter flair, and much more.

The King Cobra, shown in Bright Red (Code 2R) with optional "T-Roof" Convertible, also has all the power you want. It includes a 5.0 litre (302 CID) 2V V8 engine, 4-speed floor shift, power front disc brakes, power steering, raised white letter radial tires and Rallye Package which includes extra cooling, heavy duty springs, adjustable shock absorbers, rear stabilizer bar and dual sport mirrors.

Other great features of the King Cobra option include:

(B) Unique snake decal. The King Cobra trademark that signifies it's a standout. And the bold black grille makes your King Cobra striking.

(C) Rear deck spoiler. A crowning touch available in a wide array of colors.

King Cobra . . . drive it at your local Ford Dealer's. You'll then see why it's called King!

(D) Cobra II. For that exhilarating feeling! The Cobra II option is available on the 4-passenger 2+2 and includes the following great features:

□ Front/rear deck spoilers □ Black louvers on backlite and flipper quarter windows □ Tricolor racing stripes all-around □ Cobra II emblem on Blackout grille with bright surround molding □ Black dual sport mirrors □ Cobra II bodyside identification □ Styled steel wheels with trim rings □ Raised white letter radials □ Black windshield wiper arms, windshield/backlite moldings, rocker panel/upper door moldings □ Pivoting quarter windows (not available with "T-Roof" Convertible) □ Appearance hood scoop □ Rallye Package which includes heavy-duty springs, adjustable shock absorbers, and extra cooling.

Shown in White (Code 9D), the Cobra II is powered by a 2.3 litre overhead cam engine and 4-speed manual transmission with floor shift. Both are standard.

Note: See Notable Standard Features, Measurements and Color Code References on back cover.

Some items shown are optional, such as four white lacy spoke aluminum wheels, and bumper guards.

(B)

(C)

(D) Mustang II Cobra II

FUNCTIONAL

- 2.3 litre 2V overhead cam, 4-cylinder engine (Hardtop, Ghia, 2+2) DuraSpark Ignition
- 4-speed fully synchronized manual transmission floor-mounted shift
- Rack and pinion steering
- Turn signal mounted windshield wiper/washer controls
- Front disc brakes
- Color-keyed urethane bumpers
- Tachometer and fuel/ammeter/temperature gauges
- Hand-operated parking brake with warning light
- Antitheft Door Lock Plungers
- Fold-down rear seats/liftgate (2+2, Mach 1)
- Dual sport mirrors (Mach 1, Rallye Appearance Package, Cobra II, King Cobra)
- Rear stabilizer bar

- BSW steel-belted radial ply tires (Ghia), BSW bias ply tires (Hardtop), bias belted RWL or WSW tires (2+2), raised white letter wide-oval steel-belted radials (Mach 1)
- Ford Motor Company Lifeguard Design Safety Features

APPEARANCE AND COMFORT

- Low-back bucket seats with all-vinyl trim
- Integral door armrests
- 10-oz. cut-pile carpeting
- Pecan woodtone appliques (Hardtop, Ghia), brushed aluminum appliques (2+2, Mach 1)
- Sport Steering Wheel (2+2)
- Argent grille (Hardtop, Ghia), Blackout grille (2+2, Mach 1)
- Bright windshield, rear window, drip and belt moldings
- Full wheel covers (4) (Hardtop)
- Styled steel wheels (4) (2+2)
- Front spoiler (2+2)

Ghia has all the above with these additions:
- Color-keyed deluxe belts
- Luxury all-vinyl seat trim
- Luxury Decor door trim panels with large armrests
- Deluxe parking brake boot with rear ashtray
- Half-vinyl roof
- Opera windows
- Pinstripes
- Color-keyed vinyl insert bodyside moldings
- Ghia ornamentation
- Deluxe wheel covers (4)

Mach 1 has most of the above with these differences:
- 2.8 litre 2V V-6t
- Black lower bodyside/back panel/paint/tape treatment
- Bright lower bodyside molding
- Styled steel wheels with trim rings (4)
- Mach 1 identification
- RWL tires

†N.A. on high altitude area cars.
For content of optional packages, see pages 14, 15.

	Wheelbase	Length	Height	Width	Tread Front/Rear		Trunk Space	Fuel Capacity	Curb Weight	Passenger Capacity
HARDTOPS	96.2"	175.0"	50.3"	70.2"	55.6"	55.8"	6.7 cu. ft.	13 gals.	2,712 lbs.	4
3-DOORS	96.2"	175.0"	50.0"	70.2"	55.6"	55.8"	22.8 cu. ft.*	13 gals.	2,756 lbs.	4

*Cargo volume index

CORROSION PROTECTION. Ford takes steps to see that your new car is engineered and built to high quality standards. And in order to keep your car looking new, we incorporate the use of galvanized steel and other precoated steels, vinyl sealers, aluminized wax in critical areas, and enamel as a finishing coat.

REDUCED SCHEDULED MAINTENANCE. As part of a continuing program to lower your cost of ownership, scheduled maintenance on Ford Mustang II has been reduced steadily since 1974. For example, with the 1978 Ford Mustang II, you can now go 12 months or 10,000 miles between scheduled oil changes and 30,000 miles between lubes. These are just two small parts of the comprehensive scheduled maintenance reduction program which, in total, lowers your cost of ownership by an estimated 60% or $300 on the 1978 Ford Mustang II, equipped with a 2.8 litre engine and automatic transmission. Computations are based on Ford's Labor Time Standards, a $14.50 hourly labor rate and manufacturer's suggested retail parts prices, effective May 19, 1977.

OPTION AVAILABILITY. Some features presented are optional at extra cost. Some options are required in combination with other options. Availability of some models and features described may be subject to a slight delay. Ask your Ford Dealer for the latest information on options, prices and availability.

PRODUCT CHANGES. Ford Division reserves the right to change specifications any time without incurring obligations.

REPLACEMENT PARTS. Be sure to specify genuine Ford-approved parts and Autolite Spark Plugs from Motorcraft.

FORD
MUSTANG II

FORD DIVISION

FORD
When America needs a better idea, Ford puts it on wheels.

For Mustang fans, 1979 was a "coming home" year. The "II" appendage to the Mustang name was abandonned with little sense of loss and a Mustang that was an all-new product with several exciting performance packages made its debut (with the exception of three basic engines and transmissions and the use of the Cobra name as an option package). Four versions were offered, beginning with a two-door notchback priced at $4,071. A hatchback version listed for $4,436. The higher trim level Ghia models were priced respectively at $4,642 and $4,824.

The new model, which was destined to serve as the basis for Mustangs up to the present time, was designed according to the perception that a true total performance automobile combined superior handling, above average acceleration capability and efficient use of its overall size into a well-balanced, aerodynamic package. In regard to this latter point, the Mustang had one of the lowest drag coefficients of any American production automobile at that time. A total of 136 hours in the University of Maryland wind tunnel resulted in a 0.46 drag coefficient for the two-door notchback Mustang and a 0.44 figure for the three-door hatchback version. Among the key contributors to the Mustang's slippery shape were flush-mounted side windows, a sharply sloped windshield and front hood-grille region. The influence of Jack Telnack, who had previously served as Ford of Europe's design vice-president prior to returning to the U.S. as executive director of North American Light Car and Truck Design in early 1975, furthered the influence of European automobile philosophy upon the Mustang.

Overall, the 1979 Mustang's appearance was highlighted by a very restrained use of chrome and a high degree of functionalism. Both the front and rear bumpers were well integrated into the body's basic form and a 360 degree rub-strip, interrupted only by wheel cut-outs served both a practical purpose and as a key styling factor. Emphasizing the Mustang's attractive styling was the $175 Sport Option with its black window frames, belt moldings and rocker panel trim. The wrap-around body side molding and bumpers were fitted with dual accent stripes and trim rings and black hub caps were installed on steel wheels. When compared to the Mustang II, its successor had a longer by 4.2 inches wheelbase of 100.4 inches. Its 179.1 inch overall length exceeded that of the Mustang II by 4.3 inches. Overall height was now 51.6 inches and width was measured as 67.4 inches. These changes allowed significant improvements to be made in the Mustang's interior space accommodations yet its approximate curb weight of 2,750 lbs. with a 302 cid V-8 represented a weight reduction in the neighborhood of 200 lbs.

Carried over from the Mustang II were the 1978 model seats, which still lacked a backrest angle adjustment. However, they were reshaped with added padding for more lateral restraint. A Fairmont dash was used, but the Mustang was fitted with a zero to 8000 rpm tachometer, dials for oil pressure, coolant temperature, fuel level, and ammeter. A trip odometer was also included. Among the numerous interior options available for the Mustang, those of interest to performance oriented customers included the four-way manually adjustable driver's seat ($35), leather wrapped steering wheel (price range $41-$53, depending on model), tilt steering column ($69) and leather-vinyl upholstery ($282). A console option listing for $140 included a digital clock with month and date readings, as well as a graphic display in the shape of an automobile that alerted the driver to

brake or lighting failure and low fuel or windshield washer levels.

Ford's mid-sized Fairmont, which had earlier received good reviews from the motoring press, provided the Mustang with its basic floorpan and steering/suspension components. Coil springs were used at all four wheels with a modified MacPherson strut front suspension which placed the coil spring between the lower control arm and a longitudinal member. A four-link suspension arrangement was used at the rear. In addition, two suspension options were offered. A $33 handling package consisted of a rear stabilizer bar, stiffer springs and shocks plus firmer suspension bushings. Its purchase required the installation of 14 inch radial tires in place of the standard 13 inch bias ply units. Their prices ranged from $43 to $209 depending upon the model under consideration.

Far more exotic was the TRX option offered for any 1979 Mustang. It was based upon Michelin TRX 190/65R-390 tires and special forged-aluminum rims with dimensions of 15.4 inch (diameter) and 5.9 inch (width). With single-ply sidewall cords plus steel and Kevlar belts, these tires' ability to maintain a perpendicular position relative to the road under high lateral stress was excellent. Mustangs with this option and the base 2.3 liter four cylinder engine were equipped with a 0.50 inch rear stabilizer bar. Those with either of the 2.6 liter V-6s had 0.56 inch rear bars and V-8 powered Mustangs were given an even larger diameter 0.62 inch stabilizer bar. All TRX Mustangs had special springs and shock rates. The cost of the TRX option depended upon the model on which it was installed. A typical price was $570.

Equally alluring were the Mustang's optional engine offerings for 1979. The base 2.3 liter four-cylinder was credited with 88 hp at 4400 rpm. The German-built 2.8 liter V-6 was given a new cam and free-flowing exhaust manifold for the 1978 model year and was rated at 109 hp at 4800 rpm. Available on all models except those with the Cobra option for $273, it was initially offered only with the automatic transmission. Later in the year, Ford's Mexican-built four-speed overdrive manual gearbox (redesigned with an internal shift linkage) could be ordered with this engine. However, this combination also was short lived since a scarcity of V-6s prompted Ford to replace them with an 85 hp, 200 cid in-line six.

Listing for $514 was Ford's 302 cid V-8, which was moderately redesigned for 1979. Its overall weight was reduced by 21 lbs., due in part to a new aluminum water pump. In addition, its overall length was shortened by ½-inch. Replacing three separate belts was a single, fiberglass-reinforced flat belt that operated all accessories. Mustangs with this engine, which developed 140 hp at 3600 rpm, were equipped with 10.1 inch front disc brakes and rear drum brakes measuring 9x1.75 inches.

Technically the most interesting (and at $542, the most expensive) Mustang engine option was the 2.3 liter turbocharged four cylinder. Fitted with a Garrett AirResearch TO3 turbo limited to a maximum boost of 6 psi, its peak horsepower was 131 at 5400 rpm. The only transmission offered with this engine was a Borg-Warner four-speed.

Identification of a turbo-engined Mustang wasn't difficult. Bright "Turbo" lettering was carried on a non-functional hood scoop and a similar instrument panel applique identification was installed. In addition, two dash-mounted lights monitored the turbo's performance. A green light operated whenever the turbo was providing boost and both a red light and buzzer were activated if the boost exceeded 6 psi.

Either the 302 V-8 or turbo-charged four were available in the $1,173 Cobra option. Other technical features included the TRX tire-suspension package, a sport-tuned exhaust with bright tail pipe extensions, the semi-metallic front brake pads and rear aluminum brake drums.

Exterior body identification consisted of color-keyed rear quarter louvers, black paint and tape on grille, lower body side and below the front and rear bumpers, dual color-keyed rub strip inserts, black window molding and side body "Cobra" labels. The Cobra hood graphic was listed as a separate $78 option. Highlighting the Cobra equipped Mustang's interior were engine turned panels for the dash with a Cobra emblem on the passenger's side. Ghia level door inserts were also used with additional appliques.

Ford provided Mustang pace cars for the Indianapolis 500 powered by 260 hp 302 V-8s and to mark the occasion some 11,000 "replicas" with either production version 302 V-8s or turbo four cylinder engines were produced. With orange, red and black decorations on a black and pewter finish, plus front and rear spoilers as well as a sun roof, these Mustangs were not for shy types!

The overall Mustang package was further refined and upgraded for 1980. New standard equipment included P-metric radial tires, halogen headlights and cars powered by engines other than the base 2.3 liter (140 cid) in-line unit were equipped with semi-metallic brake linings. All Mustangs had their interior door releases moved to a higher, more convenient location and, as an option, Recaro seats with infinitely adjustable backrests and open-mesh headrests were offered. A cargo area cover for three-door models also was available.

Both the 2.3 liter four cylinder and 3.3 liter six were carried over from 1979, with the turbo-charged 2.3 liter featuring rerouted fuel lines and an electric rather than engine-driven fan. Although Ford still had a 302 cid V-8 in production, it was not available for installation in a Mustang. Instead, this V-8 served as the origin of a 4.2 liter (255 cid) V-8 option for the 1980 Mustang. With approximately 130 hp and a weight some 60 lbs. less than the 302 V-8, it was available only with automatic transmission. During the model year, Ford offered both an automatic and five-speed manual transmission for either of the Mustang's four cylinder engines.

The $1,482 Cobra option with new exterior graphics, the nose design of the Indy pace car, IMSA-type front air dam and rear spoiler, hood scoop design and Marchal driving lights was once again the choice of performance-minded Ford fans.

Changes were held to a minimum for the 1981 model year. Aside from the addition of the T-Top option priced at $916, the most obvious change was the Mustang's considerably higher cost. The two-door model now listed for $6,363 compared to the $5,338 price of the 1980 version. However, an S version with a reduced equipment-trim level was offered in 1981 for $5,897.

Although Chevrolet's new Camaro with its super-smooth styling received plenty of attention, it was the Mustang GT and the return of the 302 cid V-8 in considerably more potent form that heralded the fact that in substance and spirit, if not in name, the "Boss" was back. Thus, while the Mustang's basic styling remained virtually unchanged from the

previous model, 1982 was an important year in its history.

Some enthusiasts undoubtedly bemoaned the passing of the 2.3 liter, turbocharged four, which in 1981 had risen in price to $610. The last hadn't been heard from this concept but for 1982 no excuses were needed for its temporary demise, since the $8,303 Mustang GT could stake out a legitimate claim as one of America's fastest accelerating cars. The 302 HO (High Output) engine which made this possible developed 157 hp at 4200 rpm and 247 ft-lb of torque at 2400 rpm. On all key points its superiority to the previous 302 V-8 offered in the Mustang was apparent. Its cam had more lift, duration and overlap and a double row roller timing chain replaced the standard link single chain used previously. In addition, nickel chrome exhaust valves with flash-chromed stems were installed, along with a more powerful (8.5 instead of 6.5 psi) fuel pump. The HO engine's aluminum intake manifold carried a two-barrel, 356 cfm Ford carburetor which represented a good step forward from the 310 cfm two-barrel used in 1979. Some critics might have found fault with the GT's non-functional hood scoop, but a closer look underneath revealed that it served an important purpose since it provided room for the spun aluminum air box-filter unit from the 351 cid LTD HO police engine package to be installed. In addition, the 302 V-8's front cover and water pump were cast aluminum and the ribbed aluminum rocker arm covers carried "Powered by Ford" lettering.

Supporting this impressive engine was a cast of outstanding components. A four-speed, wide-ratio transmission was standard, as was a 3.08 Traction-Lok rear axle, power disc/drum brakes and steering. An interesting feature of the GT handling package was a bar which attached to the axle housing. Under hard acceleration this element came into contact with the lower control arms, thus limiting wheel hop. Other components included P185/75R14 blackwall steel radial tires, cast aluminum wheels, stiffer front stabilizer bar, rear stabilizer bar and revised ratings for springs, bushings and shock absorbers. For an additional $105, the TR Performance Suspension option was offered for the Mustang GT with P190/650R-390 TRX low-profile steel-belted radials, forged metric aluminum wheels and special handling components.

The Mustang's superior performance was predicted by its exciting exterior. Only three colors (red, black and metallic silver) were available and all moldings, trim, door handles, mirrors as well as the radio antenna were given a black finish. Painted in the GT's body color were its nose, grille, front air dam (which enclosed twin fog lamps), rear spoiler, headlight doors, cowl and lower back panel applique. Enhancing the GT's appearance and providing on-demand open air motoring was the optional, at $1,021, T-roof.

Key features of the GT interior, which was offered in either a red or black finish, included full instrumentation (with a tachometer red-lined at 6000 rpm), blackout trim for the dash, knobs and controls, as well as a 4-spoke steering wheel. In addition, the center console carried a graphic display warning module and an electronic, digital clock providing day, date and elapsed time information. Recaro seats listing for $834 could be ordered in place of the standard, low-back, fully reclining bucket seats.

Ford continued to keep the pressure on the Mustang's competitors in the resurging high performance market in 1983. Styling changes were limited to a reshaped front end and restyled taillights with a two-tiered horizontal format. The net result was a 2.5% reduction in overall drag. The GT's external appearance was now dominated by a black hood section that was joined by a blacked-out grille. GT identification was found on the forward hood section and above the 5.0 engine designation on the lower front fenders. Included in the GT's base price of $9,445 was a more powerful 175 hp engine fitted with a Holley four-barrel, a less restrictive exhaust system and a 17 inch (instead of 15 inch) diameter air cleaner.

As a warm-up act for the 1984 SVO Mustang, a 2.3 liter turbo charged four cylinder engine returned to the Mustang's engine line-up as a 1983½ option. Standard with this engine was a five-speed manual gearbox (also available for the GT) and a 3.45:1 Traction-Lok rear axle.

Ford was not, however, neglecting the Mustang's roadability and handling. The GT suspension was updated by shock absorbers with 50% stiffer rebound damping, a larger rear anti-sway bar and 20% faster steering. The TR option now included larger TRX 220/155HR-390 tires.

Rounding out the Mustang's performance sports car personality for 1983 was the first soft top Mustang in a decade, the four-passenger GLX convertible.

With 1984 and the availability of the Turbo GT and SVO models, Ford placed the Mustang in the forefront of high performing American automobiles.

Although the basic Mustang body was six years old, its appearance in SVO (Special Vehicle Operations) form belied its age. The only SVO identification appeared on the left rear deck, but the use of special design features for the SVO made any other labels superfluous. A flush front end with a small opening above the bumper, single rectangular halogen lights, a functional off-set hood scoop and an air dam with integral fog lamps were unique to the SVO in the Mustang line-up. Just in case anyone missed the SVO's entry onto the American road, they had a second chance to identify this outstanding automobile by virtue of the small fairings fitted to the rocker panels head of the rear wheels, the double level polycarbonate black rear spoiler and the SVO's special 16x7 cast aluminum wheels with their flush aerodynamic design.

The SVO's interior was equally satisfying to behold. A full complement of dials and gauges, backlighted by red-orange lighting, included a 0-8000 rpm tachometer with a 6000 rpm red line. An interesting feature was a zero to 140 mph speedometer with numerals only up to the 85 mph level! Additional instrumentation of the SVO dash, with its charcoal finish, included a turbo boost gauge reading from zero to 18 psi, which operated in conjunction with an overboost warning light and buzzer. Steering column levers were provided for the interval windshield wipers, lane-change/directional signals and the headlight flash-to-pass feature. A three-hole leather-wrapped steering wheel derived from a Ghia show car with six tilt positions was standard, as was a leather covering for the shift boot, shifter and emergency brake handle.

Since the SVO was a sophisticated world-class grand touring automobile, its interior included both functional features such as a pedal package allowing for heel-and-toe downshifting-braking, with a footrest next to the clutch pedal and such convenience features as vanity mirrors placed in both sun visors, a swiveling reading light at the windshield top and a center console incorporating an armrest, non-lockable storage area with rocker

switches for the fog lamps. A premium AM/FM stereo sound system incorporating four speakers and a 25 watt power amplifier was also standard SVO equipment.

The SVO's all-cloth front bucket seats were multi-adjustable and equipped with inflatable lumbar supports operated by a pump located in the front corner of the seat. Leather seat inserts were optional. The rear seats were of a new split-fold down design. When both were lowered, over 32 cubic feet of storage were available.

With 175 hp at 4500 rpm and 210 ft-lb of torque at 3000 rpm, the turbo-charged, electronic fuel-injected SVO 2.4 liter, sohc four cylinder engine was the antithesis of the big-engined Mustangs from earlier years. However, its potency and design sophistication placed it in the forefront of two decades worth of great Mustang powerplants. An intercooler located between the turbocharger and intake manifold reduced the temperature of the intake charge from 300 degrees Fahrenheit to 175, thus increasing its density for added power. An electronic boost control operated by a dash-mounted switch allowed either premium or regular unleaded fuel to be used.

A standard five-speed overdrive transmission with a Hurst-designed shift linkage delivered the SVO's power to a 3.45:1 axle with a Traction-Lok differential. Providing the SVO with superior cornering power was a front suspension system with an additional one inch of travel and by the use of Lincoln Continental forged lower control arms, revised geometry. Adjustable ("Cross Country," "GT," or "Competition") Koni low-pressure, gas-filled shock absorbers were fitted at all four wheels. Beginning late January 1984, the rear traction bars were replaced by horizontally mounted shock absorbers positioned between the rear axle ends and the frame. The SVO's cast aluminum wheels carried Goodyear 225/50VR-16 NCT radials and vented disc brakes (10.9 inch front, 11.3 inch rear) were installed.

A somewhat tamer 2.3 turbocharged engine was also available on a limited basis for the GT Mustang. However, the most common engine under the GT's black band hood was the 5.0L High Output V-8. This engine was linked to a Borg-Warner five-speed manual, while a less powerful (165 hp to 205 hp) 302 cid V-8 was offered with a four-speed automatic overdrive transmission. At mid-year, the GT rear suspension received the same four-shock setup as did the SVO.

Debuting as a special 1984½ Mustang was the limited edition 20th Anniversary model available in Turbo GT form and as either a convertible or hatchback. These special edition Mustangs celebrated the April 17, 1964 introduction date of the original Mustang via a white exterior complete with GT-350 tape stripes and a front fascia with the original Mustang horse ornamentation. The interior, with a canyon red finish, also featured a 20th anniversary instrument panel applique and each buyer of the approximately 5,000 anniversary Mustangs built received a personalized plate with the vehicle's serial number.

The new 1979 models were well-launched, indeed, when they were selected to pace the Indianapolis 500. A two-panel magazine ad was prepared to commemorate this event (see pages 104-105). Excerpts from the 1979 Mustang catalogue appear on pages 106-115. Excerpts from the 1980 Mustang catalogue appear on pages 116-123. Excerpts from the 1981 Mustang catalogue appear on pages 124-131. Excerpts from the 1982 Mustang catalogue appear on pages 132-137. Excerpts from the 1983 Mustang catalogue appear on pages 138-141. Excerpts from the 1984 full-line Ford catalogue appear on pages 142-143.

"I know Ford built or powered cars have won most major performance events in the world.

But the one they're proudest of is this specially modified

1979 FORD MUSTANG.

Chosen as the Official Pace Car of the 1979 Indianapolis '500'...

Gentlemen, start your engines."

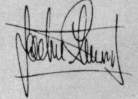

On race day the Mustang Pace Car will be driven by Jackie Stewart. He holds the world's record for number of Grand Prix victories...27. Twenty-five of these wins were chalked up in Ford-powered cars.

The official Mustang Pace Car has been mechanically modified to pace the Indy "500". For a limited time you can buy a replica of this impressive car (excluding mechanical modifications) equipped with a long list of standard features, including Recaro® seats, flip-up open air roof, Michelin TRX tires, metric forged aluminum wheels and a choice of 5.0 litre V-8 or 2.3 litre Turbocharged engine.

See your Ford Dealer and test-drive an exciting replica of the Indy Mustang today.

FORD MUSTANG

FORD DIVISION Ford

Mustang 2-Door with Sport Option and Turbocharged engine

Opt for this beauty and, as shown above in lower Tu-Tone Light Chamois (83) over Black (1C), your special 2-Door with Sport Option not only wears a front opening hood scoop (ornamental) with bright TURBO letters. It also features sport tuned exhaust with bright dual tailpipe extension. And Turbo instruments, including: 8,000 rpm tach, audible overboost and engine oil temperature warning signals. All this, in addition to the full instrumentation standard on all Mustangs: tach, trip odometer and fuel/temperature/oil pressure/ alternator gauges.

To look further into building your own kind of Mustang 2-Door, check out the full list of standards on the back cover, your interior choices (pages 12 and 13) and your optional equipment choices (pages 16-19). Then see your Ford Dealer for a test drive.

(A) Mustang 2-Door with Sport Option (details on page 6), in vibrant Yellow (64), shows off its style, highlighted here by the new wraparound taillamps.

(B) Turbo hood scoop (ornamental) is a telltale sign of the Turbocharged 2.3 litre Four that lurks within for all Mustangs. Standard on Cobra.

(C) Steering column-mounted stalk system, standard on all Mustangs, includes controls for wiper/washer and turn signal/horn/headlamp dimmer. Puts vital driving aids at your fingertips.

(D) Mustang 2-Door with Sport Option and Turbocharged engine, in Tu-Tone Light Chamois (83)/Black (1C). Shown with standard wheel covers.

Note: See Notable Standard Features, Measurements and color code reference on the back cover. Some items shown are optional. See options list on pages 16-19.

*Not available with automatic transmission or with High Altitude Emission System.

(D) Mustang 3-Door Ghia

Outside, a unique rear deck medallion distinguishes your Mustang as a luxurious Ghia. So do the color-keyed louvers and window frames. Dual remote control styled mirrors. Rocker panel moldings. And turbine wheel covers.

Underneath it all, Ghia sports all the standard Mustang features, like 2.3 litre overhead cam Four with 4-speed floor-mounted manual transmission, rack and pinion steering, front disc brakes and front stabilizer bar. They team with a suspension system, new for Mustang, to help put pure excitement back into driving.

However you look at it, and whatever additional luxuries you may find on pages 16 through 19, the new breed of Mustang Ghia may very well be the sporty, luxurious car you've been hoping to find. Test-drive one today and find out for sure.

(A) Mustang 2-Door Ghia exhibits your exquisite taste with classic understated elegance. Shown here in Black (1C), with Chamois vinyl roof.

(B) Fold-down rear seat, standard on 3-door Mustangs, folds flat to provide 32.4 cu. ft. of cargo area for everything from golf bags for your foursome, to camping gear for your family.

(C) Ghia door map pockets keep maps and other driving paraphernalia neatly at your fingertips.

(D) Mustang 3-Door Ghia, shown in Medium Grey Metallic (1P), brings you Ghia luxury plus the versatility of a third door liftgate that opens wide for easy access to the cargo area.

Note: See Notable Standard Features, Measurements and color code reference on the back cover. Some items shown are optional. See options list on pages 16-19.

FORD MUSTANG COBRA

Sporty appearance is only half of its good news.

For some cars that call themselves "sporty," appearance is everything. Literally. But fear not, for the '79 Cobra is here and better days are ahead. Days of driving fun that maybe even you thought were beyond your dreams.

The new breed of Cobra rolls out sporting the new 2.3 litre Turbocharged overhead cam Four.* Teamed with a slick-shifting 4-speed manual transmission and 3.45 rear axle ratio to keep you coiled and ready to strike out for parts known or unknown at the slightest provocation.

We think the new breed of Cobra will demonstrate a degree of roadability that should make a believer out of you, no matter how roadwise you are. Thanks to a combination of Mustang's traditional handling features *plus* a special suspension system to go with Cobra's Michelin TRX tires and forged metric aluminum wheels. Cobra also has front disc brakes with new semi metallic pads and aluminum rear brake drums.

Inside, Cobra treats you to all the special Mustang standards *plus* distinctive Black engine-turn design instrument panel applique and ribbed

door trim insert with Cobra insignia. And three-spoke Sport steering wheel.

Outside, Cobra sports a look that's sure to get looks wherever you go (see back cover for full details).

Now that you know what the '79 Mustang with Cobra Option is, it's time to try it.

(A) Mustang 3-Door Cobra in Silver Metallic (1G) features an optional Flip-Up Open Air Roof. The color-keyed louvers and Black accents tell you this is no ordinary breed of car.

(B) Cobra with hood graphics in colors that best coordinate with your Cobra's body color, like the Black with Orange

and Yellow accents, shown on this Bright Red beauty (2P).

(C) Cobra Instrument panel. The look is unmistakably sporty. And, as with all Mustangs, fully instrumented: tach, trip odometer, fuel/temperature/oil pressure/ alternator gauges.

Note: See Notable Standard Features, Measurements and color code reference on back cover.

Some items shown are optional. See options list on pages 16-19.

*Not available with automatic transmission or with High Altitude Emission System.

(A) Mustang 3-Door Cobra

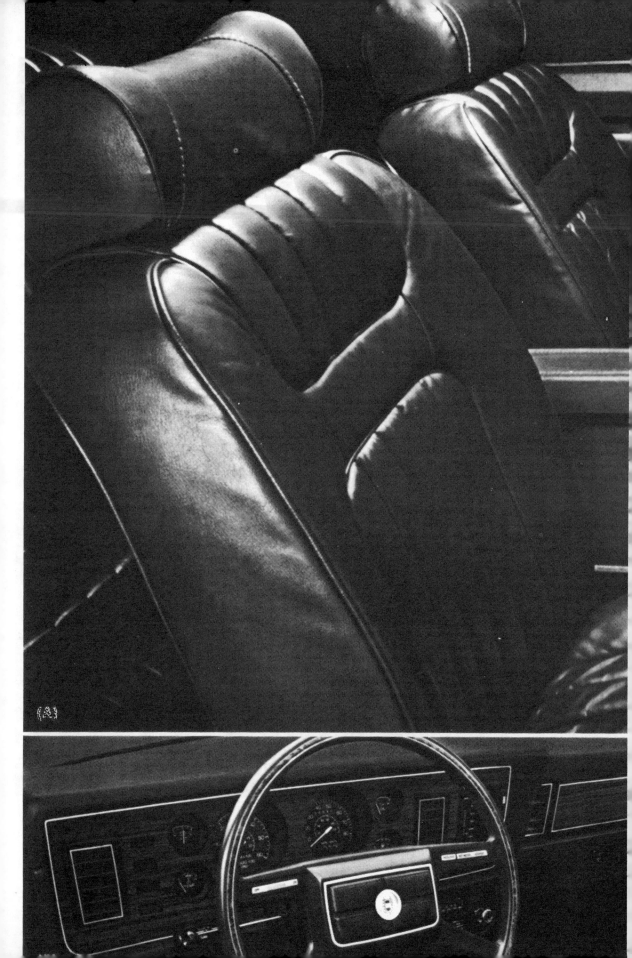

FORD MUSTANG
INTERIORS
Match your personality.

Now that you've pretty much settled on the style of Mustang that best suits the kind of driver you are, it's time to choose the style of interior that best reflects the kind of individual you are. And what a choice: fabulous new fabrics, captivating new colors, striking new styles . . . positive proof that Mustang's beauty *is*—indeed—more than skin deep.

electronic digital clock with date and elapsed time numeric display.

(B) Driver's-eye view of Ghia's fully instrumented control panel graphically illustrates the fact that it was designed with the driver in mind. Tach, trip odometer and fuel/temperature/oil pressure/ alternator gauges tell you precisely what your Ghia is up to. All controls are easy to read and reach. And the full-width woodtone applique adds a handcrafted look that rivals the more expensive makes. Shown here, in place of the standard

(C)

(E)

(D)

(F)

(A) Genuine leather and vinyl trim option, shown on top-of-the-line Ghia buckets, is also available for Cobra. Also as an optional part of the Interior Accent Group. Shown in new Vaquero (EZ), also yours in White, Black, Chamois, Red and Medium Wedgewood Blue. Also shown is optional console which features: built-in cigarette lighter, ashtray and map/glove box; graphic warning module that alerts you to fluid and lamp outages;

Sport steering wheel, is the deluxe 4-spoke steering wheel that comes with optional fingertip speed control.

(C) Interior Accent Group features low-back buckets with optional check-pattern cloth and vinyl upholstery. Here in Black (DA). Also in Red, Medium Wedgewood Blue, Chamois and Vaquero, all with White background. Or, you can choose the handsome crinkle-grain vinyl trim that's standard (D). Or, you can opt for genuine leather and vinyl trim (A).

This optional accent group, offered on all Mustangs except Ghia, also adds: passenger side visor vanity mirror, inertia seat back release, color-keyed deluxe belts with tension eliminator, Deluxe Sound Package and carpeted luggage compartment (2-door).

(D) Interior Accent Group, here with low-back buckets trimmed in standard crinkle-grain vinyl. Or you can opt for the check-pattern cloth/vinyl trim (C). Shown in Chamois (CT), this good-looking trim is also yours in White, Black, Red, Medium

console), is far from plain. With trimmings you don't have to pay extra for, like: full door trim with bright hardware and moldings, padded upper panel, carpeted lower portion and deluxe steering wheel (Sport steering wheel shown).

(F) Standard all-vinyl for the high-back buckets of Cobra (shown) and standard 2-Door or 3-Door. This good-looking pebble-grain pattern and all its easy-care advantages can be yours in Black (AA), as shown, or White, Chamois, Red, Vaquero and Medium Wedgewood Blue.

(G)

Wedgewood Blue or Vaquero.

(E) Houndstooth cloth/vinyl trim for Mustang's standard high-back buckets. The sporty looking bold pattern of this optional trim is available for all Mustangs, except Ghia. Distinctive in new Medium Wedgewood Blue (BB), also available in Vaquero, Red, Black or Chamois. Pebble-grain vinyl (see "F") is standard. And, as you can plainly see, Mustang's standard interior (shown with optional

(G) Ghia Interior, featuring low-back buckets with European-style headrests trimmed in optional velour-cloth and vinyl upholstery. An elegant exclusive with top-of-the-line Ghia, this choice is yours as shown in Red (FD), Chamois, Black, Vaquero or Medium Wedgewood Blue. Crinkle-grain vinyl is standard.

Note: Some items shown are optional. See options list on pages 16-19. Color code reference is on the back cover.

Mustang Choices

Mustang 2-Door, Medium Vaquero Glow (5W)

Mustang 3-Door, Medium Blue Glow (3H)

Mustang 2-Door with Exterior Accent Group*
Light Medium Blue (3F)

Mustang 2-Door with Sport Option,*
Tangerine (85)

Mustang Ghia 2-Door, Medium Grey Metallic
(1P)

Mustang Ghia 3-Door, Light Chamois (83)

Mustang Cobra 3-Door,* Yellow (64)

Notable Standard Features

MUSTANG 2-DOOR/3-DOOR

FUNCTIONAL

■ 2.3 litre 2V overhead cam, 4-cylinder engine
with DuraSpark Ignition
■ 4-speed, fully synchronized, manual transmission
with floor-mounted shifter
■ Rack and pinion steering
■ Front disc/rear drum brakes
■ Strut front suspension/4-bar link rear suspension
■ Front stabilizer bar
■ 13-in. bias ply tires (BSW)
■ Dual rectangular headlamps
■ Wraparound taillamps
■ Fluidic windshield washers
■ Full instrumentation: tachometer, trip odometer,
fuel/temperature/oil pressure/alternator gauges
■ Steering column-mounted 2-lever system:
1. Windshield wiper/washer
2. Turn signal/horn/headlamp dimmer
■ Anti-theft door lock plungers
■ Hand-operated parking brake with warning light
■ Inside hood release
■ Glove box lock
■ Day/night rearview mirror
■ Passenger door courtesy light switch
■ Cigarette lighter
■ Continuous loop belts
■ Unitized body construction
■ Ford Motor Company Lifeguard Design Safety
Features

APPEARANCE AND COMFORT

■ High-back bucket seats with all-vinyl trim
■ Deluxe cut-pile carpeting
■ Full door trim with padded upper panel, bright
moldings and carpeted lower panel
■ Full-width woodtone instrument panel appliques
■ Deluxe steering wheel (2-door), Sport steering
wheel (3-door)
■ Flat luggage floor, full mat, insulation package

Measurements

	Wheelbase
2-DOOR	100.4"
3-DOOR	100.4"

†12.5 gal. on standard 2.3 litre Four with SelectAire Conditioner,

Notes

CORROSION PROTECTION. Ford takes steps to see
that your new Mustang is engineered and built to
high quality standards. And in order to keep your
Mustang looking new we incorporate the use of
precoated steels, such as galvanized steel and
chrome/zinc-rich primer-coated steel, vinyl sealers
aluminized wax in critical areas, and enamel as a
finishing coat.

REDUCED SCHEDULED MAINTENANCE. As part of
a continuing program to lower the cost of ownership,
scheduled maintenance requirements on most new
Fords have been reduced dramatically in recent
years. For example, with the new 1979 Ford Mustang,

- Fold-down rear seat/liftgate (3-door)
- Color-keyed louvers (2-door), Black (3-door)
- Color-keyed door and window frames with bright moldings (2-door)
- Black-painted door and window frames, belt and rocker panel moldings (3-door)
- Bright windshield, drip, side and rear window and headlamp moldings
- Black left-hand rearview styled mirror
- Black cowl molding, windshield wipers, grille and lower back panel
- Soft urethane-covered front and rear ends
- Color-keyed bumpers with Black rub strips (2-door), plus dual accent stripe inserts (3-door)
- Wide Black bodyside moldings with dual accent stripe inserts (3-door)
- Full wheel covers, 2-door (4)
- 13-in. Sport wheels, 3-door (4)

MUSTANG GHIA

Most standard Mustang 2-Door features, plus these additions or variations:
- Low-back buckets with European-style headrests
- Color-keyed deluxe belts
- Luxury cut-pile carpeting
- Ghia door trim with badge, soft inserts, map pockets and carpeted lower panels
- Sport steering wheel
- Light Group (see page 16 for full details)
- Roof-mounted passenger-assist grab handle
- Right-hand visor vanity mirror
- Ghia sound package
- Carpeted luggage compartment (2-door)
- Ghia insignia on deck lid/third door
- Color-keyed window frames, louvers and dual remote control styled mirrors
- Bright belt and rocker panel moldings
- Pin stripes

- Wide Black bodyside moldings with dual color-coordinated accent stripe inserts
- Dual color-coordinated accent stripe inserts on bumpers
- Turbine wheel covers (4)
- 14-in. steel-belted (BSW) radial ply tires

MUSTANG COBRA*

Most standard Mustang 3-Door features, plus these additions or variations:
- 2.3 litre Turbocharged engine**
- TURBO instrument panel lights, audible overboost and engine oil temperature warning system
- 8,000 rpm tachometer
- Black engine-turn design applique on instrument panel
- Cobra insignia on instrument panel and ribbed door trim insert
- Color-keyed side window louvers
- Front opening hood scoop (ornamental), bright TURBO nameplate
- Cobra door decal (hood graphics, optional)
- Black window frames, moldings and lower body
- Wide Black bodyside moldings with dual color-coordinated accent stripe inserts
- Bright dual tailpipe extension
- Michelin 190/65R 390 TRX (BSW) tires
- 390 mm-15.35-in. Forged metric aluminum wheels (4)
- Special suspension system with heavy-duty front and rear stabilizer bars, special shock valving
- Aluminum rear brake drums and semi-metallic front disc brake pads
- 3.45 axle ratio

*For content of optional packages, see pages 5, 6, 7, 10, 11. See options list on pages 16-19.

**Not available with automatic transmission or with High Altitude Emission System.

Length	Height	Width	Tread Front/Rear	Trunk or Cargo Volume	Fuel Capacity	Curb Weight	Passenger Capacity
179.1"	51.5"	69.1"	56.6"/57.0"	10.0 cu. ft.	11.5 gals.†	2,516 lbs.	4
179.1"	51.5"	69.1"	56.6"/57.0"	32.4 cu. ft.	11.5 gals.†	2,550 lbs.	4

2.3 litre Turbo, 2.8 litre V-6; 16.0 gals. with 5.0 litre V-8.

the recommended maintenance schedule is 10,000 miles (7,500 miles with V-8 engines), or 12 months (on V-6 engines and most I-4 engines), between scheduled oil changes and 30,000 miles between lubes. These are just two small parts of the comprehensive program, which, in total, can significantly lower the cost of scheduled maintenance for Mustang over 50,000 miles of driving.

COLOR AND TRIM CODES. Car colors and trims are coded, example: Tangerine (85). Your Ford Dealer will be pleased to show you color samples of paint and trim materials.

OPTION AVAILABILITY. Some features presented are optional at extra cost. Some options are required in combination with other options. Availability of some models and features described may be subject to a slight delay. Ask your Ford Dealer for the latest information on options, prices and availability.

PRODUCT CHANGES. Ford Division reserves the right to change specifications any time without incurring obligations.

REPLACEMENT PARTS. Be sure to specify genuine Ford-approved parts, Motorcraft Parts and Autolite Spark Plugs from your Ford Dealer.

FORD MUSTANG

Sports car styling, 3-door versatility.

When you think of a sports car, pure driving enjoyment comes to mind. But you needn't be a sports car enthusiast to appreciate the fun of driving a Mustang. With the Mustang herd you run free in your own personal style.

The versatile 3-door model is a fine example of Ford's Better Ideas for the 80's. You have Mustang's sleek, aerodynamic styling and engineering value (see pages 14-15). Plus the long list of standard features detailed on page 15, including those in the Sport Option: black window frames and rocker panel moldings, wide wraparound bodyside molding with dual argent stripe inserts, 13-in. sport wheels/trim rings, sports steering wheel.

Sporty styling and appointments are part of the picture. Add the 3-Door's spacious 33.3 cu. ft. of cargo area (rear seat down), and you have a car that meets your practical needs, too.

(A) Mustang 3-Door in Medium Grey Metallic (1P)* with optional 2.3 liter turbocharged engine. Ford offers the only 4-cylinder turbo engine built in America.

(B) Mustang 3-Door in White (9D)* with optional turbocharged engine and accent tape stripes.

(C) Standard 2.3 liter OHC 4-cylinder engine accounts for Mustang's excellent fuel economy.† Comes with sporty 4-speed floor-mounted manual transmission; optional SelectShift automatic transmission available.

(D) The 2.3 liter turbocharged engine has acceleration comparable to some other cars with V-8 engines. Plenty of reserve power for passing or freeway merging. The turbocharger is basically an air compressor driven by recycled exhaust gases. At your command, it pressurizes atmospheric air to increase the velocity of the fuel/air mixture. This simple principle produces great acceleration.

Note: See Notable Standard Features and Measurements on page 15, and color code reference on back cover.
Some items shown are optional. See options list on pages 16-17.
*All models except Cobra and Carriage Roof option have bright window moldings.
†See mileage statement on page 3.

(B) Mustang 3-Door with Turbocharged Engine and Accent Tape Stripes

Atmospheric Air   Pressurized Air

Exhaust to Turbo   Exhaust from Turbo

(C)   (D)

Your personal sporty 2-door.

Mustang 2-Door has special appeal all its own. It's a great personal car, designed for your style of driving with Ford's Better Ideas for the 80's. And it's our lowest-priced Mustang.

The 2-door model offers a lot for your money. Consider the many standard features you get. Like new P-metric steel-belted radial tires, high-illumination halogen headlamps, maintenance-free battery. Comfortable high-back bucket seats. An instrument panel with woodtone appliques and full instrumentation, including tachometer and trip odometer. Plus so much more.

And beneath its sporty, aerodynamic styling lines are Mustang's outstanding engineering features on pages 14-15. Like the modified MacPherson strut front suspension, 4-bar link coil spring rear system, rack and pinion steering.

Best of all, our lowest-priced Mustang provides excellent fuel economy with its standard 2.3 liter OHC 4-cylinder engine and 4-speed manual transmission.† And there's also the 2.3 liter turbocharged engine, which delivers acceleration comparable to some other cars with V-8 engines. See page 5.

(A) Mustang 2-Door with Sport Option with Tu-Tone paint in striking Light Medium Blue (3F) over Black (1C).* Included are: wide wraparound body-side molding with dual argent stripe inserts, black window frames and rocker panel moldings, 13-in. sport wheels with trim rings. And a sports steering wheel.

(B) New Carriage Roof option. ‡Gives convertible look to Mustang 2-Door in Bright Caramel (5T).

(C) Mustang 2-Door with Sport Option, shown here in Bright Red (27).*

(D) Mustang 2-Door in Bright Yellow (6N).* Very stylish. The only options shown are Exterior Accent Group (pin stripes, black rocker panel moldings and rub strip extensions, bumper rub strip accent stripes) and whitewall tires.

Note: See Notable Standard Features and Measurements on page 15, and color code reference on back cover.

Some items shown are optional. See options list on pages 16-17.

*All models except Cobra and Carriage Roof option have bright window moldings.

† See mileage statement on page 3.

‡ See your Ford Dealer for availability.

(B) Mustang 2-Door with Sport Option, new Carriage Roof and Turbocharged Engine

(C) Mustang 2-Door with Sport Option

(D) Mustang 2-Door with Exterior Accent Group

FORD MUSTANG
COBRA

(A) Mustang

3-Door Cobra

Bold new expression of our sports car for the 80's.

Mustang 3-Door Cobra strikes a new image of sportiness in 1980.

New styling features—Indy 500 Pace Car front end with integral spoiler and dual fog lamps, unique rear-opening hood scoop (non-functional), rear deck spoiler, exclusive tape stripe treatment. Plus blackout greenhouse moldings, remote control styled mirrors, black lower Tu-Tone paint. These hint at what Cobra is under its gleaming hood. *Turbocharged!*

The 2.3 liter turbo engine comes standard on Cobra. At first you won't believe you're driving on four cylinders as the turbo kicks in, delivering acceleration comparable to some other cars with V-8 engines. Acceleration you can use for passing or freeway merging. For more on turbocharging, see page 5.

Also included on Cobra is a special suspension system with Michelin TRX tires mounted on 390 mm (15.3-in.) forged metric aluminum wheels.

We call Cobra the boldest of the Mustang breed. For reasons that speak well for themselves.

(A) Mustang 3-Door Cobra in Black (1C), shown with eye-catching Cobra hood graphics, optional. The unique rear-opening hood scoop (non-functional) adds much to Cobra's super sporty styling.

(B) Mustang 3-Door Cobra in Bright Caramel (5T). Inside, Cobra comes with turbo instrumentation: 8000-rpm tach, audible overboost and engine oil pressure monitoring system. Plus black engine-turned instrument panel appliques. All in addition to Mustang's standard interior features (page 15).

(C) New integral front spoiler with dual fog lamps. The Indy 500 Pace Car look here tells immediately of the excitement you're to experience in Cobra.

(D) Rear deck spoiler, another new sporty Cobra attraction for 1980.

Note: See Notable Standard Features and Measurements on page 15, and color code reference on back cover.
Some items shown are optional. See options list on pages 16-19.

(B) Mustang 3-Door Cobra

(C)

(D)

9

In the tradition of elegant, sporty cars.

Ghia is the elegant member of the Mustang herd. Youthful and carefree, with many luxury refinements.

Ghia is indeed distinctive, as our display models reveal. Full wraparound bodyside molding with dual color-coordinated accent stripe inserts. Dual remote control styled mirrors. Bright rocker panel moldings. Dual accent pin stripes. Color-keyed window frames and rear pillar louvers. 14-in. turbine wheel covers. Plus a Ghia insignia on decklid or liftgate.

No less luxurious is Ghia's interior. Low-back bucket seats with European-style headrests and inertia seat back releases, luxury door trim with soft insert appliques, medallion, carpeted lower panels and map pockets shown on page 12(A). Plus deluxe belts with tension eliminators, deep cut-pile carpeting, RH visor vanity mirror and roof-mounted assist handle. Also, carpeted luggage compartment (2-door), Deluxe Sound Package, and the Light Group items on page 17.

With all of this luxury, Ghia packs the performance of the economical 2.3 liter engine/4-speed manual transmission powerteam,† one of Mustang's many Better Ideas for the 80's.

(A) Mustang 3-Door Ghia, 4-passenger seating with third door loading and carrying versatility, in White (9D).

(B) Mustang 3-Door Ghia in Dark Cordovan Metallic (8N). A fine combination of sportiness and luxury.

(C) Mustang 2-Door Ghia will move you with classic elegance. Shown in Silver Metallic (1G) with Black vinyl roof.

(D) Ghia's luxury door trim with map pockets is but one of many elegant appointments.

(E) 3-door cargo area has 33.3 cu. ft. of usable load-carrying capacity with the rear seat down. Carpeted cargo floor is standard on all 3-door models.

Note: See Notable Standard Features and Measurements on page 15, and color code reference on back cover.
Some items shown are optional. See options list on pages 16-19.
†See mileage statement on page 3.

(B) Mustang 3-Door Ghia

(C) Mustang 2-Door Ghia

(D)

(E)

11

FORD MUSTANG
ENGINEERING

Here's where our Better Ideas for the 80's begin:
AN INSIDE LOOK AT FORD MUSTANG

A. Modern Aerodynamic Design. Aerodynamic efficiency means less wind resistance, which can help improve performance and fuel economy.

B. Suspension System. Up front, a modified MacPherson strut-type suspension with stabilizer bar. In the rear, a 4-bar link suspension with coil springs.

C. Economical 2.3 Liter OHC 4-Cyl. Engine. This standard Mustang engine (except Cobra) features overhead cam design, Holly-Weber staged 2V carburetor with crossflow design of intake and exhaust ports. Available in turbocharged version, which provides acceleration comparable to some other cars with V-8 engines.
(See mileage statement on page 3. More on the turbocharger, page 5.)

D. Responsive Front Disc Brakes resist fade because they dissipate heat more effectively, are less affected by rain and dampness. Incorporate audible wear sensors.

E. Precise Rack and Pinion Steering. A direct, low-friction system which provides steering response with minimal effort.

F. New P-Metric Steel-Belted Radial Ply Tires. Standard on all Mustangs (see Notable Standard Features on next page for sizes). Major feature is higher inflation pressure for reduced rolling resistance. Shown are optional Michelin TRX 190/65R 390 metric tires.

G. Fully Synchronized 4-Speed Manual Transmission. Companion to the standard 2.3 liter and optional 2.3 liter turbocharged 4-cylinder engines. Fully synchronized to permit rapid upshifting and downshifting at moderate speeds without gear clash. Includes sporty short-throw shift lever.

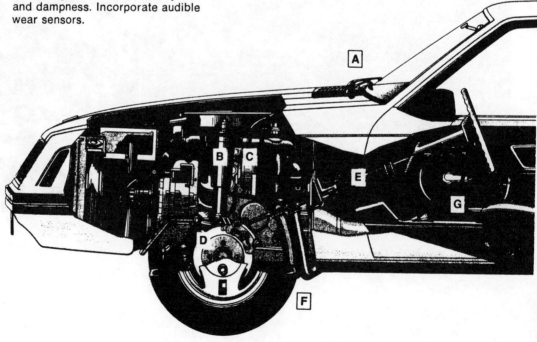

Mustang's major design and engineering features represent a modern approach to what driving is about for the 1980's—a design concept that offers you traditional Ford value with today's emphasis on efficiency.

H. Spacious Interior Design. Efficient use of interior space is one of Mustang's great features. Mustang's design offers a lot of room for a car of its size. Compared with its predecessor, the New Breed Mustang has up to 3 in. more front shoulder room, 2 in. more front hip room, 5 in. more rear leg room, 4 in. more rear shoulder room, and 6 in. more rear hip room.

I. Solid Unitized Body Construction. Mustang's unitized body is a one-piece steel shell with smooth-fitting seams. Front suspension strut attaching points and engine front-mounting brackets are integral with fender aprons.

J. Flat Luggage Compartment Floor is a design feature of the New Breed Mustang. Gives the 2-Door almost 2 cu. ft. more luggage capacity than its predecessor; gives the 3-Door with rear seat folded down over 5 in. more cargo floor length and 9 cu. ft. more carrying capacity.

Plus These Additional Features: Column-mounted control 2-lever system. New high-illumination halogen headlamps. New maintenance-free battery. Fluidic windshield washer system. Combination wiper solution/coolant overflow reservoir. Seal-on-body door weatherstrip system. And more.

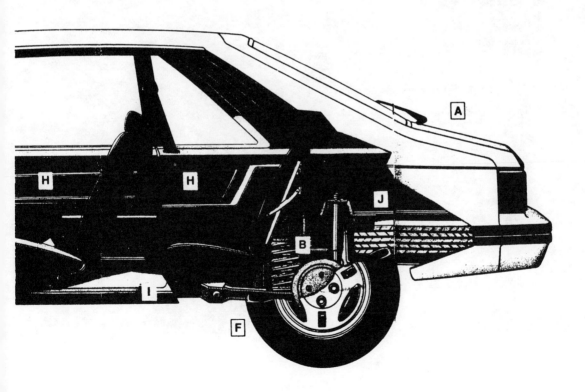

Ford
MUSTANG
PERFORMANCE

Here's where Mustang really shines. Mustang performance is backed by proven engineering features like manual or power-assisted rack and pinion steering. Modified MacPherson strut front suspension. Front disc/rear drum braking and P-metric radial tires. All this wrapped in a sleek exterior that was developed and shaped in the wind tunnel.

Mustang gives you a choice of eight different engine/transmission combinations. Included is a turbocharged 2.3 liter with 5-speed manual overdrive.

Combine Mustang's performance characteristics with Ford engineering and you have one great car.

Mustang's rack and pinion steering and trim, sporty size ease the job of maneuvering in and out of tight parking spaces. For even more convenience, there's a variable ratio power steering option that gives all the benefits of rack and pinion plus the additional ease of power steering.

Mustang takes the curves with modified MacPherson strut suspension and stabilizer bar up front. A four-bar link coil spring setup in the rear completes the system, all specially tuned for use with radial ply tires. There's also a Handling Suspension option (standard on Cobra) that includes revised shock absorber valving, stiffer front stabilizer bar, stiffer rear springs and a rear stabilizer bar.

Mustang's fun-to-drive attitude is complemented by its standard fuel-efficient 2.3 liter OHC 4-cylinder* and 4-speed manual transmission. Or you can have the 2.3 liter turbo option that delivers plenty of reserve power whenever you call for it. You can move up in engine size with the 3.3 liter (200 CID) in-line Six or the 4.2 liter (255 CID) V-8.

Mustang's corrosion protection is enhanced through the use of precoated and galvanized steel panels and the increased use of non-corroding high-strength plastics. And Ford backs it up with a 3 year, unlimited mileage, corrosion perforation warranty (see page 13 for details).

We could go on and on about Mustang's performance qualities, but you should experience them for yourself with a test drive—see your Ford Dealer today.

See Mustang Data Center (pages 12 and 13) for Notable Standard Features, Measurements and EPA information* Some items shown are optional; see Options Selector for a complete list (pages 14 and 15).

5

Ford
MUSTANG
GHIA
THE MUSTANG WITH
ALL THE LUXURY TOUCHES

(A) Mustang Ghia 2-Door

(B) *Mustang Ghia 3-Door*

Mustang Ghia. Refreshing. like a sea breeze in full sails. Ghia will lift your spirits and carry you with distinctive pride and elegance.

Ghia, in 2- or 3-door models, includes refined exterior touches like dual black remote control mirrors, bodyside pin-stripes and turbine wheel covers. Inside there are Ghia's low-back reclining buckets with adjustable headrests, deluxe seat belts with tension elim-inators, and luxury level cut-pile carpeting. Ghia also includes pivoting map/dome light and lights for ashtray, glove box. engine compartment, and trunk. Plus a lot more (pages 12-13).

(A) Mustang Ghia 2-Door with Black Carriage Roof, in Tu-Tone Light Pewter Metallic (1T) over Black (1C).

(C)

(D)

(B) Mustang Ghia 3-Door with Flip-Up Open Air Roof, in Red (24).

(C) Low-back buckets in Medium Red optional fine-ribbed cloth (FD).

(D) Low-back buckets in Pewter with optional ultra-soft leather seating surfaces (EP).

See Mustang Data Center (pages 12 and 13) for Notable Standard Features, Measurements and EPA Information. Some items shown are optional; see Options Selector for a complete list (pages 14 and 15).

Ford
MUSTANG
COBRA
THE MUSTANG THAT SPEAKS PERFORMANCE

Mustang Cobra. The free-spirited, bold, daring Mustang. Cobra is for those special people who appreciate and seek out performance excellence.

From its front end treatment with air dam, fog lights and rear opening (non-functional) hood scoop to the integral rear spoiler, Cobra speaks performance. Cobra backs up its bold stance with a turbocharged 2.3 liter OHC 4-cylinder and the Handling Suspension System which includes adjusted

shock absorber valving, stiffer front stabilizer bar, stiffer rear springs and rear stabilizer bar. Michelin's ultra-low profile TRX steel-belted radials mounted on forged aluminum metric wheels round out one beautiful system. All the above are standard, of course.

In Cobra's command driving position, you look out over full instrumentation that includes an 8,000 RPM tach and a turbo monitoring system.

Fully reclining high-back bucket seats are standard. But if you want the ultimate, you can wrap yourself in the reclining Recaro buckets (an option) with their special orthopedic design.

10

(A) Mustang Cobra

(B) Mustang Cobra

(C)

(A) Mustang Cobra in Polar White (9D).

(B) The bold Cobra at left is shown in Bright Bittersweet (2G) and sports the optional eye-catching tricolored hood graphics in Red.

(C) Recaro seats in Black cloth (TA) feature a stationary headrest design, excellent shoulder, side, and thigh support with an insertable wedge for additional lower back support.

See Mustang Data Center (pages 12 and 13) for Notable Standard Features, Measurements and EPA information. Some items shown are optional, see Options Selector for a complete list (pages 14 and 15).

11

Audio

- AM Radio with Dual Rear Seat Speakers
- AM/FM Monaural Radio
- AM/FM Monaural Radio with Dual Rear Seat Speakers

(A) AM/FM Stereo Radio*

(B) AM/FM Stereo Radio* with Cassette Tape Player. Uses space-saving 60-minute compact cassette tapes.

- AM/FM Stereo Radio* with 8-Track Tape Player
- Premium Sound System. For all stereo radio/tape systems. Includes premium rear speakers and extra-power amplifier.

*Dual speakers, front and rear, included.

Appearance

- Cobra Option (see pages 10-11). Note: Tape treatment may be deleted for an individualized Cobra.
- Cobra Hood Graphics

(C) Flip-Up Open Air Roof. Opens part way for ventilation or can be removed to bring in fresh air and sunshine.

- T-Roof. New for '81. Remove one or both sections depending on how much of the great outdoors you want to bring indoors. Shown on cover, pages 2-3, 4-5. Both open air roof and T-Roof include storage bags for carrying roof panels.

(D) Black Liftgate Louvers (3-Door)

- Deluxe Luggage Rack (roof-mounted)
- Dual Remote Control Mirrors
- LH Remote Control Mirror
- Metallic Glow Paint. Available in Medium Blue Glow (3H) and Bittersweet Glow (8D).
- Special Tu-Tone Paint Treatment. Available in Dark Cordovan Metallic/Bittersweet Glow; Medium Pewter Metallic/Light Pewter Metallic; Red/Polar White; Midnight Blue Metallic/Medium Blue Glow.
- Lower Tu-Tone Paint Treatment. Black lower bodyside. (Standard on Cobra.)
- Carriage Roof. The look of a classic convertible. Offered on 2-Door in White, Black, Blue or Brown grained vinyl. Shown on page 9.
- Full Vinyl Roof (2-Door). Available in White, Black, Medium Red, Light Pewter, Midnight Blue, Dark Brown, Bittersweet.
- Sport Option (2-Door). Includes sport wheel treatment, black window frames and rocker panel moldings, sport steering wheel.
- Accent Tape Stripes. Bodysides and decklid/liftgate.
- Pinstripes. On the bodysides and decklid/liftgate.
- Hood Scoop. Front opening (non-functional).

Comfort

(E) SelectAire Conditioner. With manual controls to regulate cooling, heating, fresh air, defrosting and defogging for year-round comfort. Tinted glass recommended.

- Interior Accent Group. Includes: deluxe sound package, fully reclining low-back bucket seats in higher level vinyl, inertia seat back releases, full wrapover soft luxury door trim panels, deluxe seat belts with tension eliminators, passenger visor vanity mirror, and carpeted luggage compartment (2-Door).
- Tinted Glass—Complete
- Recaro Seats. (See page 11 for details.)

Convenience

- Color-Keyed Deluxe Belts with Tension Eliminators
- Electric Rear Window Defroster. Quickly removes snow, ice, frost or condensation from rear window.
- Fingertip Speed Control. Allows you to cruise the highway more relaxed with your foot off the accelerator. All controls mounted in steering wheel spokes.

(F) Leather-Wrapped Sport Steering Wheel (shown). Leather-Wrapped Luxury Steering Wheel also available.

- Tilt Steering Wheel
- Light Group. Pivoting map light, ashtray and glove box lights, plus engine and luggage compartment (2-Door) lights. Includes a third door courtesy light switch on 3-Door models.

(G) Console. Conveniently arranged system, featuring electronic digital clock with elapsed time and date; graphic display warning module that indicates low-fuel/low-washer fluid level and warns you if headlamp low beam/rear running lamps/brake lamps are out. Also includes built-in cigarette lighter, ashtray and map/glove box.

- SelectShift Automatic Transmission
- 5-Speed Manual Overdrive Transmission.* Overdrive gear reduces engine RPM, helps improve fuel economy.
- Interval Windshield Wipers
- Cargo Area Cover (3-Door models)

Interiors (for seats and trims, see model pages)

Performance

- 2.3 Liter Turbocharged Engine. Includes turbo instrumentation: 8000-rpm tach and turbo monitoring system. Plus sport-tuned exhaust, 3.45 axle ratio, heavy-duty battery, rear-opening hood scoop (non-functional) with bright "Turbo" letters, and instrument panel turbo identification.
- 3.3 Liter (200 CID) "I" 6-Cyl. Engine. Includes 4-speed manual overdrive transmission.
- 4.2 Liter (255 CID) V-8 Engine. Includes variable venturi carburetor in California.
- Higher axle ratios. 3.08 and 3.45 (only with 2.3L and 4.2L engines with auto. trans.)
- Traction-Lok Axle.* Automatically transfers power to the wheel with the most traction.
- Heavy-Duty Maintenance-Free Battery (optional with 3.3L, 4.2L and California Emission System).
- California Emission System. Required in California. Includes variable venturi carburetor on 4.2 liter (255 CID) V-8 engine.
- Sport-Tuned Exhaust. With bright tailpipe extension. Included with 2.3 liter turbo engine and manual transmission.
- Handling Suspension. Includes larger front stabilizer bar, rear stabilizer bar (except with 2.3 liter engine), adjusted spring and bushing rates and shock valving.
- Michelin TRX Tires. Low-profile Michelin 190/65R 390 TRX tires are mounted on matched optional 390 mm (15.3-in.) forged metric aluminum wheels.

*See your Ford Dealer for availability.

Ford Mustang
OPTIONS SELECTOR

(A)

(B)

(E)

Selecting options for your new Mustang can be doubly rewarding. With your selection, you can _personalize_ your Mustang. And by adding to the actual dollar value in the beginning, options can contribute to your trade-in value when it's time for another new Mustang. The '81 Mustang options list is as varied as it is long. See for yourself.

(C)

(D)

(F)

Power Assists

- Power Front Disc Brakes
- Power Side Windows: new for 1981
- Power Lock Group. Includes power door locks, power decklid/liftgate release.
- Variable Ratio Power Steering

Protection

- Rear Window Washer/Wiper (3-Door)
- Rocker Panel Moldings
- Appearance Protection Group. Includes: front deluxe carpet floor mats, door edge guards, and front and rear license plate frames (if needed).
- Mud/Stone Deflectors.
- Lower Bodyside Protection. Provides an application of vinyl under the paint along the lower sides of the body. Important on gravel and heavily salted roads.

Tires

- List of available tires ranges from 13- and 14-in. metric-sized radial ply tires to metric 390 mm/15.3-in. low-profile TRX tires. Select black or white sidewall (BSW/WSW) or raised white letters (RWL). Except TRX.

(H) Wheel Covers/Wheels
From top: Turbine Wheel Covers (4), Wire Wheel Covers (4), Cast Aluminum Wheels (4), Styled Steel Wheels with Trim Rings (4), Forged Metric Aluminum Wheels (4).

Options Availability

1981 Mustang options are not confined to these pages but are shown throughout the catalog. Options, whether or not they are identified, are offered at extra cost. Some options are offered only in combination with other options. Availability of some models and features described here and elsewhere may be subject to delay. Again, consult your Ford Dealer for the latest information.

(G)

(H)

THIS IS FORD **MUSTANG** FOR 1982.

Right: Mustang GL 3-Door shown on pages 2-3, front and back cover.

R. center: Mustang GLX 2-Door shown originally on pages 6-7.

A spirited answer to today's driving needs.

Since its introduction in September, 1978, the new-design Mustang has dominated the small specialty car segment of the American market with over 634,000 sales!* It's easy to see why. Mustang is a highly efficient mode of transportation and it gets you where you're going in style. Mustang makes you feel good.

Mustang for '82 comes in two body styles, the more formal notchback 2-door with conventional rear seat or the racy-looking fastback 3-door with fold-down rear seat (and cargo space for over 32 cu. ft. of gear). There are four levels of Mustang fun for you to choose from: L, GL, GLX and GT. Pick any one of them and you'll be putting Mustang spirit into your lifestyle.

*Based on R.L. Polk registrations from October, 1978, through May, 1981, with adjustments to exclude sales of prior model year Mustang II's reported after October 1, 1978.

MUSTANG L (2-Door only)

Mustang L comes with a standard 2.3 liter OHC 4-cylinder engine and these impressive EPA estimates: 32 est. hwy. and 22 EPA est. mpg** Add a fully synchronized 4-speed manual transmission with self-adjusting clutch, and you're ready for some driving fun.

Modified MacPherson strut front suspension is up front with a 4-bar link coil spring suspension setup in the rear. Rack and pinion steering provides a quick and precise steering response while a front stabilizer bar helps reduce body roll through the corners.

**Projected Ford Division estimates for comparison. Your mileage may differ depending on speed, distance and weather. Actual highway mileage will probably be lower. See your Ford Dealer for his 1982 EPA Gas Mileage Guide.

Manual front disc brakes combine with rear drums for sure quick stops on P-metric 14-inch radial ply tires.

A full wraparound bodyside molding system is more than a styling element; it helps protect Mustang's sleek exterior from parking lot dings and dents. A black styled left-hand rearview mirror is remote controlled for added driver convenience.

The L's sporty interior features reclining high-back bucket seats in vinyl or optional cloth and vinyl. There's full sports instrumentation that includes a 6000 RPM tachometer and trip odometer with gauges for oil pressure, coolant temperature and alternator charging.

Two steering column-mounted levers place the turn signals, horn, headlamp dimmer, windshield washer and wipers at your fingertips. Mustang L's standard offerings go on to include cut-pile carpeting, soft wrapover door trim panels that provide comfortable armrests with integral door pull handles plus theft-proof door lock buttons, deluxe seat belts with comfort regulators, and more (see Notable Standard Features, pages 16-17).

MUSTANG GL

GL is the intermediate series in Mustang's hot '82 lineup and it doesn't give an inch in either style or comfort. Racy blackout trim accents the window frames, quarter window louvers and rocker panels. Pinstripes on the upper bodysides provide additional highlights. Turbine wheel covers add further distinction to this series.

The sporty flavor of GL carries over into the interior with a sport steering wheel plus low-back reclining bucket seats in all-vinyl or optional cloth and vinyl. Or seat yourself on real leather seating surfaces (an option).

There's also color-keyed carpeting on lower door trim panels. The luggage compartment in the 2-door is carpeted, and the 3-door features a carpeted load floor plus carpeting on the rear seat back.

MUSTANG GLX

This is the top-of-the-line Mustang that turns heads as neatly and surely as it takes corners.

GLX exterior features dual color-keyed accent stripe inserts in the bodyside molding and bumpers plus dual accent bodyside pinstripes. Dual bright remote control mirrors and bright rocker panel moldings help distinguish and complement GLX's sleek exterior.

Interior luxury is equally appealing with fully reclining low-back bucket seats trimmed in vinyl (your choice of nine color schemes). You also have your choice of optional cloth and vinyl or, for the ultimate feel of luxury, ultra-soft leather and vinyl (shown on pages 4-5). Mustang GLX's quiet elegance is carried through soft wrapover luxury door trim panels, carpeted on the lower sections. For convenience, a map pocket is included on the driver's side. Deep cut-pile carpeting further enhances the look and feel of GLX's warm and inviting interior. A luxury steering wheel adds a separate note of sports elegance. Courtesy lighting is provided with an overhead dual beam map/dome light, plus lights for ashtray and glovebox as well as engine compartment and trunk light (2-door) or third door courtesy light switch (3-door).

L. center: Mustang L 2-Door shown on pages 8-9.

Left: Mustang GT shown originally on pages 10-11.

MUSTANG GT

If excitement is your master key, this Mustang opens all the doors. The front view alone tells you this one means business. Note the fog lamps, low-slung air dam and spoiler. The air dam isn't just for looks either. It works by directing air flow around the sides rather than under the car. This helps reduce lift pressure and drag on under-body components. A rear spoiler adds a racy look to the body treatment and creates a downward force on the rear end at highway speeds.

A special beefed-up suspension system gives the GT a stiffer, sportier ride. It includes a stiffer-than-standard front stabilizer bar, rear stabilizer bar, adjusted spring and bushing rates, and adjusted shock absorber valving. Wide P185/75R-14 steel-belted radials put more rubber on the road for a wide, bold stance.

Blackout treatment highlights the GT interior from the ignition switch to the door lock buttons.

An electronic digital day/date/elapsed time clock and graphic display warning module are incorporated into the GT console. The module contains warning lights that signal low levels for fuel or windshield washer solvent, or if a headlamp, taillamp or brake lamp needs replacement.

Interior comfort is high level with low-back reclining buckets, luxury cut-pile carpeting and soft wrapover door trim panels carpeted on the lower sections. If you want the ultimate in driving comfort, you can wrap up in optional Recaro buckets. Recaro seats with their orthopedic design are recognized by many experts as among the best available.

Any way you look at it, this is a great going Mustang. If you want to make it even more so, consider the optional high-output 5.0 liter V-8. For more details, see pages 14-15.

FORD **MUSTANG** DATA CENTER

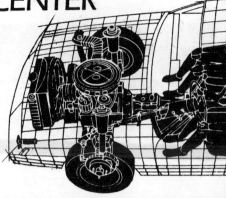

FORD LIMITED CORROSION PERFORATION WARRANTY

Mustang, like all new model Ford cars sold in the 50 United States, is covered by Ford Motor Company's 3-year, unlimited mileage corrosion perforation warranty. Under this warranty any part which, in normal use, rusts through from corrosion within three years of retail delivery or first use will be repaired or replaced free of charge by the selling dealer after inspection by a Ford representative. Exhaust system components or parts which develop corrosion perforation as a result of accidents or other damage are not covered.

FORD-PAID REPAIR PROGRAMS AFTER THE WARRANTY PERIOD

Sometimes Ford offers adjustment programs to pay all or part of the cost of certain repairs. These programs are intended to assist owners and are in addition to the warranty or to required recalls. Ask Ford or your dealer about such programs relating to your Ford or Lincoln-Mercury vehicle.

To get copies of any adjustment program for your vehicle or the vehicle of interest to you:

Call Ford toll-free at 1-800-241-3673. Alaska and Hawaii call 1-800-243-3711 and in Georgia call 1-800-282-0959.

Or write Ford at:

Ford Customer Information System
Post Office Box 95427
Atlanta, Georgia 30347.

We'll need your name and address; year, make, and model vehicle, as well as engine size; and whether you have a manual or automatic transmission.

NOTABLE STANDARD FEATURES

ENGINEERING	L	GL	GLX	GT
2.3 liter OHC 4-cylinder (140 CID) engine	S	S	S	S
DuraSpark electronic ignition	S	S	S	S
Electronic voltage regulator	S	S	S	S
Maintenance-free battery (45 amp-hr.)	S	S	S	S
4-speed manual transmission	S	S	S	S
Self-adjusting clutch linkage	S	S	S	S
3.08:1 rear axle ratio	S	S	S	S
MacPherson strut-type front suspension	S	S	S	S
4-bar link/coil spring rear suspension	S	S	S	S
Front stabilizer bar	S	S	S	S
Handling suspension system*	O	O	O	S
Front disc brakes	S	S	S	S
Rear drum brakes	S	S	S	S
Rack and pinion steering	S	S	S	S
P175/75R 14 BSW steel-belted radial ply tires	S	S	S	NA
P185/75R 14 BSW steel-belted radial ply tires	O	O	O	S

EXTERIOR				
Dual rectangular halogen headlamps	S	S	S	S
Dual fog lamps	NA	NA	NA	S
Full wraparound bodyside molding protection system	S	S	S	S
Black rocker panel moldings	NA	S	NA	NA
Bright rocker panel moldings	O	NA	S	NA
Black left-hand remote control mirror	S	S	NA	S
Black right-hand remote control mirror	O	O	NA	S
Dual bright remote control styled mirrors	NA	NA	S	NA
Front air dam	NA	NA	NA	S
Rear spoiler	NA	NA	NA	S
Full deluxe wheel covers	S	NA	NA	NA
Turbine wheel covers	NA	S	S	NA
Cast aluminum wheels	O	O	O	S

INTERIOR				
... instrumentation**				
... steering column-mounted controls for turn signals, horn, headlamp dimmer				
... windshield wipers and fluidic washer system				
Cigarette lighter				
AM radio w/dual front speakers (may be deleted for credit or upgraded at extra cost)				
Inside hood release				
Day/night rearview mirror				
Fully reclining high-back bucket seats with inertia seat-back latches in all vinyl				
Fully reclining low-back bucket seats with inertia seat-back latches in all vinyl	NA			
Color-keyed cut-pile carpeting				
Fold-down rear seat w/one-hand operation and color-keyed carpeted seat back (3-door only)	NA			
Color-keyed carpeted load floor (3-door only)				
Carpeted luggage compartment (2-door only)				
Trim Group				
Console				

S = Standard,   O = Optional,   NA = Not Available

*See options selector for complete description.
**... in addition to speedometer and odometer, resettable trip odometer, fuel, temperature, oil pressure and voltage charging gauges, plus 6,000 RPM tachometer.

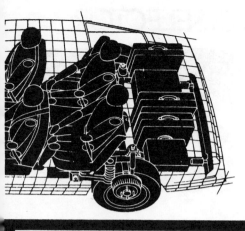

MEASUREMENTS

	2-Door/3-Door
Wheelbase	100.4"
Length	179.1"
Height	51.5"
Width	67.4"
Tread: Front/Rear	56.6"/57"
Trunk or cargo volume	10.0/32.7 cu. ft.*
Fuel Capacity	15.4 gal.
Curb Weight	2,619/2,656
Passenger capacity	4

*With rear seat down.

COLORS AND TRIMS

INTERIOR TRIM COLORS	EXT. PAINT COLORS	Black	Polar White	Silver Metallic	Medium Grey Metallic	Red	Bright Red	Medium Blue Glow*	Dark Blue Metallic	Pastel Vanilla	Medium Vanilla	Bittersweet Glow*	Medium Yellow	Dark Curry Brown Metallic	Dark Cordovan Metallic
Black		X	X	X	X	X	X			X	X	X	X		
Medium Red		X	X	X	X	X	X								
Medium Wedgewood Blue		X	X	X				X	X						
Vanilla		X	X							X	X		X		
Vaquero		X	X									X			X
Opal/Black		X	X	X	X								X		
Opal/Blue			X					X	X						
Opal/Red			X		X	X									
Opal/Vaquero			X									X			X

See your Ford Dealer for actual samples of colors and trims.
* Optional Glow Colors.

SCHEDULED MAINTENANCE

Ford wants to reduce both the frequency and cost of scheduled maintenance on its cars to an absolute minimum. Here are the scheduled maintenance intervals for the new Mustang.

Engine Oil Change	each 7,500 miles
Spark Plug Change	each 30,000 miles
Air Filter Replacement	each 30,000 miles
Engine Coolant Replacement	each 52,500 miles or 3 years

EPA MILEAGE ESTIMATES

32 HWY | 22 MPG

Projected Ford Division estimates for comparison. Your mileage may differ depending on speed, distance and weather. Actual highway mileage will probably be lower. See your Ford Dealer for his 1982 EPA Gas Mileage Guide.

TECHNICAL SERVICE BULLETINS

All vehicles need repairs during their lifetime. Sometimes Ford issues Technical Service Bulletins (TSBs) and easy-to-read explanations describing unusual engine or transmission conditions which may lead to costly repairs, the recommended repairs, and new repair procedures. Often a repair now can prevent a more serious repair later. Ask Ford or your dealer for any such TSBs and explanations relating to your Ford or Lincoln-Mercury vehicle.

To get copies of these Technical Service Bulletins and explanations for your vehicle or the vehicle of interest to you:

Call Ford toll-free at 1-800-241-3673. Alaska and Hawaii call 1-800-243-3711 and in Georgia call 1-800-282-0959.

Or write Ford at:

Ford Customer Information System
Post Office Box 95427
Atlanta, Georgia 30347.

We'll need your name and address; year, make, and model vehicle, as well as engine size; and whether you have a manual or automatic transmission.

"ASK YOUR FORD DEALER"

Following publication of this catalog, certain changes in standard equipment, options, prices and the like, may have occurred which would not be included in these pages. Your Ford Dealer is your best source for up-to-date information.

PRODUCT CHANGES

Ford Division reserves the right to change product specifications at any time without incurring obligations.

FORD **MUSTANG** OPTIONS SELECTOR

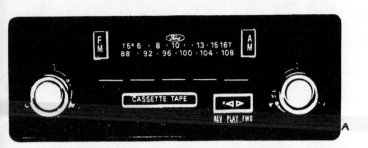

Mustang options give you the opportunity to equip your new Mustang to your personal specifications. Options add not only to the appearance, comfort and convenience of your new car, but to its overall value as well.

Audio
- AM Radio with Dual Rear Seat Speakers*
- AM/FM Monaural Radio*
- AM/FM Monaural Radio with Dual Rear Seat Speakers*
- AM/FM Stereo Radio**
- AM/FM Stereo Radio** with Cassette Tape Player (A). Uses space-saving 60-minute compact cassette tapes.
- AM/FM Stereo Radio** with 8-Track Tape Player
- Premium Sound System.* For all stereo radio/tape systems. Includes premium rear speakers and extra-power amplifier.

**Dual speakers, front and rear, included.

Appearance
- Flip-up Open-Air Roof (B).* Opens part way for ventilation or can be completely removed to bring in fresh air and sunshine.
- T-Roof (C).* Remove one or both sections depending on how much of the great outdoors you want to bring indoors. Both open air roof and T-Roof include soft vinyl storage bags for carrying roof panels.
- Black Liftgate Louvers*
- RH Remote Control Mirror
- Metallic Glow Paint. Available in Medium Blue Glow and Bittersweet Glow.
- Special Tu-Tone Paint Treatment.* See your Ford Dealer for available colors.
- Lower Tu-Tone Paint Treatment.* Black only.

- Carriage Roof (2-door only)*
- Full Vinyl Roof (2-door only)*
- Accent Tape Stripes.* Bodysides and decklid/liftgate.
- Hood Scoop. Front opening non-functional.

Comfort
- SelectAire Conditioner (D). With manual controls to regulate heating, cooling, fresh air, defogging and defrosting for year-round comfort. Tinted glass recommended.
- Tinted Glass Complete
- Recaro Bucket Seats

Convenience
- Electric Rear Window Defroster. Quickly removes snow, ice, frost or condensation from rear window.
- Fingertip Speed Control.* Allows you to cruise the highway more relaxed with your foot off the accelerator. All controls mounted in steering wheel spokes. Includes Luxury Steering Wheel. Not available with Sport Steering Wheel.
- Leather-Wrapped Steering Wheel.* 3-spoke supplied without speed control. 4-spoke supplied with speed control.
- Tilt Steering Wheel*
- Light Group. Dual beam map/dome light, ashtray and glove box lights, plus engine and luggage compartment lights (2-door) or liftgate courtesy light switch (3-door).

- Console. Conveniently arranged system, featuring electronic digital clock with elapsed time and date; graphic display warning module that indicates low-fuel/low-washer fluid level and warns you if headlamp low-beam/rear running lamps/brake lamps are out. Also includes built-in ashtray, cigarette lighter and map/glove box.
- Interval Windshield Wipers
- Rear Window Washer/Wiper (3-door)*
- Cargo Area Cover*

Performance
- 3.3 Liter (200 CID) "I" 6-Cylinder Engine*
- 4.2 Liter (255 CID) V-8 Engine*
- 5.0 Liter (302 CID) V-8 Engine*
- SelectShift Automatic Transmission (E)*
- 5-Speed Manual Overdrive Transmission (F).* Overdrive gear reduces engine RPM, helps improve highway fuel economy.
- Higher Axle Ratios (ask your Ford Dealer for details)
- Traction-Lok Axle. Automatically transfers power to the rear wheel with the most traction.
- Heavy-Duty Maintenance-Free Battery
- California Emission System. Required in California. Includes variable venturi carburetor on 4.2 liter engine.

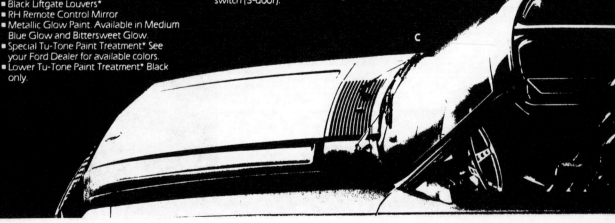

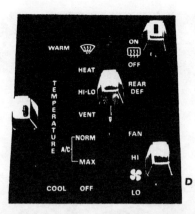

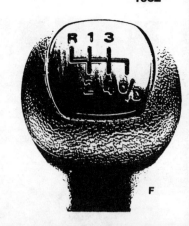

- TR Performance Suspension System. Includes larger front stabilizer bar, rear stabilizer bar (except with 2.3 liter engine), adjusted shock absorber valving and spring and bushing rates, low-profile Michelin 190/65R 390 TRX tires are mounted on matched 390 mm (15.3") forged metric aluminum wheels with anti-theft locking lug nuts.

Power Assists
- Power Front Disc Brakes*
- Power Side Windows
- Power Lock Group. Includes power door locks, power decklid release (2-door), power liftgate release (3-door).
- Power Steering Variable Ratio Design

Protection
- Rocker Panel Moldings
- Appearance Protection Group. Includes: front deluxe carpet floor mats, door edge guards, and front and rear license plate frames (if needed).
- Lower Bodyside Protection. Provides an application of vinyl under the paint along the lower sides of the body. Important on gravel or heavily salted roads.

Tires
- List of available tires ranges from 14-inch metric-size radial ply tires to metric 390 mm/15.3-in. low-profile TRX Michelin tires. Select black or white sidewall (BSW/WSW) or raised white letters (RWL). Except TRX.
- Wheel Covers/Wheels **(G)**. From top: Wire Wheel Covers* (4); Turbine Wheel Covers (4), standard on GL, GLX (see Features list, pg. 16); Forged Metric Aluminum Wheels* (4); Styled Steel Wheels with Trim Rings (4); Cast Aluminum Wheels* (4).

Also well worth considering...

EXTENDED SERVICE PLAN

Ford Motor Company's optional Extended Service Plan covers major components on new Ford cars and light trucks for longer than the vehicle's basic warranty. The cost is so moderate for the protection you get that it could pay for itself the first time you need it. Your Ford Dealer will be happy to detail the Plan for you. It is available on cars and light trucks sold and normally operated in all 50 United States and Canada.

Options Availability
This year, you can save money on the options you select for your new Mustang by choosing one or more Value Option Packages. Pick Value Package No. 253B, for example, and four options — Tinted Glass, Electric Rear Window Defroster, Fingertip Speed Control, and Tilt Steering Wheel — are included **at no extra charge.** There are seven Mustang Value Option Packages in all, each offering you two or

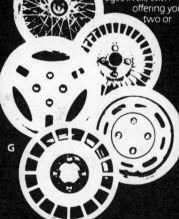

more no-extra-charge options when you buy the whole package. It's the smart, money-saving way to buy options — equipment items you'd probably select for your new Mustang anyway. Be sure to ask your Ford Dealer for all the money-saving details on Value Option Packages.

1982 Mustang options are not confined to these pages but are shown throughout the catalog. Options, whether or not they are identified, are offered at extra cost. Options designated by an asterisk (*) are offered either in combination with other options, or are subject to additional ordering requirements or limitations. Availability of some features described here and elsewhere may be subject to delay.

HE BOSS.
MUSTANG GT.
ONE HOT PIECE OF
AMERICAN STEEL
THAT JUST MIGHT
LEAVE COMPETI-
TION CHASING ITS
SHADOW.

■ Mustang GT in Bright Red with op- tional T-roof. ■ Sport steering wheel and instrumentation. ■ GT interior with op- tional Sport Perfor- mance bucket seats in Black cloth.

IT'S NOT JUST A CONVERTIBLE... IT'S A MUSTANG.*
■ Mustang GLX Convertible in Bright Red.
■ Mustang GLX Convertible in Polar White. ■ Top up — windows down — all of them, including side, quarter and even the rear zip-out glass window. And Mustang Convertibles provide fun for four. ■ Convertible low-back bucket seats in Opal vinyl.

12

*See your dealer for Mustang Convertible availability.

Ford Mustang

Little in the way of fanfare is needed to announce the new Mustangs for 1984, except to say they are "more Mustang" than ever before. There's a Mustang designed for every need, and engineered for any kind of road.

Mustang SVO

An all-new Mustang born of Ford's longtime experience in motorsports. The machine speaks for itself, with many components not found on any other production car in America. A computer-controlled 2.3 liter OHC engine with port-type electronic fuel injection, turbocharger and inter-cooler. Four-wheel disc brakes. Adjustable gas-filled Koni® shocks. Plus sports performance bucket seats, 16-inch wheels and tires, and a lot more.

Mustang GT and Turbo GT

There are two. "The Boss" is powered by a 5.0 liter High Output V-8 teamed with a 5-speed manual transmission. The Turbo GT combines 2.3 liter 4-cylinder efficiency* with on-demand electronic fuel-injected turbo performance.** Both come with special suspension packages and performance tires on cast aluminum wheels, full console, and a wide range of other sport features.

Mustang LX

Available in 2-door coupe, 3-door hatchback, or convertible. With reclining low-back front bucket seats in cloth upholstery, dual remote-control mirrors, visor vanity mirrors, luxury carpeting, LX door trim with a map pocket for the driver, special sound insulation, and much more. The LX is Mustang deluxe in every sense.

Mustang L

The standard series has the economical* 2.3 liter engine, strut-type front suspension with stabilizer bar, rack and pinion steering, halogen headlamps, LH remote-control mirror, front bucket seats and many other features. Sportiness and practicality — the standard Mustang has plenty of both.

Above Left: Mustang L 3-Door shown with optional cast metric aluminum wheels and TRX tires

Below Left: Mustang SVO

Mustang Convertibles

The Mustang GT and Turbo GT Convertible.**And the LX Convertible with electronic fuel-injected 3.8 liter V-6 and Select-Shift automatic transmission. Mustang convertible models provide room and comfort for four passengers, have a power retractable top, roll-down quarter windows, and a dual-function rear glass window that folds with the top or can be zipped out when the top is up for extra ventilation.

> *See Gas Mileage on page 19.
> **Delayed availability. See your Ford Dealer for details.
> Note: Front air dam is dealer-installed.

Below: Mustang GT Convertible shown with optional cast metric aluminum wheels and TRX tires. Front air dam is dealer-installed.

Mustang GT instrumentation. Some items shown may be optional.

Mustang L reclining bucket seats. Some items shown may be optional.

SOURCE BOOKS!

1. GTO (Bonsall)
2. Firebird (Bonsall)
3. AMX (Campbell)
4. Chrysler 300 (Bonsall)
5. Chevelle SS (Lehwald)
6. 4-4-2 (Casteele)
7. Charger (Shields)
8. Javelin (Campbell)
9. Corvette, 1953-1967 (Steffen)
10. Nova SS (Lehwald)
11. Barracuda/Challenger (Shields)
12. Roadrunner (Shields)
13. Corvette, 1968-1982 (Steffen)
14. Cougar 1967-1976 (Bonsall)
15. Trans Am, 1967-1981 (Bonsall)
16. El Camino (Lehwald)
17. Big Chevys, 1955-1970 (Lehwald)
18. Big Pontiacs, 1955-1970 (Bonsall)
19. Duster/Demon (Shields)
20. Ranchero (Ackerson)

21. Mid-Size Fords/Mercs (Ackerson)
22. Porsche 911/912 (Miller)
23. Buick Gran Sports (Zavitz)
24. Shelby, Cobras and Mustangs (Ackerson)
25. Mid-Size Dodges (Shields)
26. Ferraris of the Seventies (Ackerson)
27. Z/28 (Collins)
28. Lamborghini (Ackerson)
29. Big Fords & Mercs (Shields)
30. Jaguar XK-E (Sass)
31. Mustang (Ackerson)

CLASSIC SOURCE BOOKS

1. Mark Lincolns (Bonsall)
2. Eldorados (Bonsall)

*To be published later in 1984.

All volumes $12.95 each